PRAISE FOR *THE GATEKEEPERS: WHY SCHOOL SYSTEMS SHOULD RETINK RESISTING CHANGE*

"Barbara Smith's book provides practical insights from practitioners on the challenges of change in complex organizations. The sophisticated examples of managing the change process offer easy-to-apply strategies to help make you a more effective leader and change agent. You'll learn techniques that you can use immediately to improve your leadership by reading this book."—Lisa Gonzales, chief business officer at Mt. Diablo Unified School District, San Francisco, and former president of the Association of California School Administrators

"*The Gatekeepers* invites us to rethink the purpose of schooling, and what education might be. It acknowledges a core tension in policy—that no two schools are the same. There is potential for inequity when the rigid system does not respond to the contextual needs of those within it. Importantly, this book provides the reader with easily accessible provocations about how all educational stakeholders might create a culture of learning that inspires and reimagines current policy and practice."—Julia Morris, education researcher and visual arts education (secondary) course coordinator at Edith Cowan University, Australia

"This book offers an insightful analysis that exposes the effects of gatekeeping in education and highlights their harmful effects on schools. Barbara Smith's compelling voice sheds light on how many everyday practices are barriers in education and provides solutions for overcoming them to improve students' futures."—John Nash, author of *Design Thinking in Schools* and professor of Educational Leadership at the University of Kentucky

"*The Gatekeepers* is a great compendium of insights and avenues for changing the current education system. Whether you are inside or outside the current system read this book and 'pick your lane.' There is no greater urgency than transforming the stagnant education system."—Michael Fullan, professor emeritus at OISE/University of Toronto

The Gatekeepers

Why School Systems Should Rethink Resisting Change

Edited by

Barbara J. Smith

ROWMAN & LITTLEFIELD
Lanham • Boulder • New York • London

Published by Rowman & Littlefield
An imprint of The Rowman & Littlefield Publishing Group, Inc.
4501 Forbes Boulevard, Suite 200, Lanham, Maryland 20706
www.rowman.com

86-90 Paul Street, London EC2A 4NE, United Kingdom

Copyright © 2023 by Barbara J. Smith

All rights reserved. No part of this book may be reproduced in any form or by any electronic or mechanical means, including information storage and retrieval systems, without written permission from the publisher, except by a reviewer who may quote passages in a review.

British Library Cataloguing in Publication Information Available

Library of Congress Cataloging-in-Publication Data

Names: Smith, Barbara J., 1956- editor.
Title: The gatekeepers : why school systems should rethink resisting change / edited by Barbara J. Smith.
Description: Lanham, Maryland : Rowman & Littlefield, 2023. | Includes bibliographical references. | Summary: "The Gatekeepers is a comprehensive review of many parts of a school system that resist change. For all stakeholders to embrace improvement, they need to know what habits, practices and indifference act as barriers to growth and change. This book reveals insiders' insights into what gates exist, how to navigate around them, and why it is important to risk new ways of doing school"— Provided by publisher.
Identifiers: LCCN 2023011920 (print) | LCCN 2023011921 (ebook) | ISBN 9781475871746 (cloth) | ISBN 9781475871753 (paperback) | ISBN 9781475871760 (epub)
Subjects: LCSH: Educational change—United States. | School improvement programs—United States. | School management and organization—United States.
Classification: LCC LA217.2 .G38 2023 (print) | LCC LA217.2 (ebook) | DDC 370.973—dc23/eng/20230407
LC record available at https://lccn.loc.gov/2023011920
LC ebook record available at https://lccn.loc.gov/2023011921

This book is dedicated to those experts in education who chose to be supportive of these ideas, many I've only met through emails and LinkedIn conversations. You are not only trailblazers, but people builders making time to help people you do not even know. I dedicate this work to these precious educational leaders who have the excuse of being busy but made time anyway.

Contents

Acknowledgments ix

Introduction xi

Chapter 1: Rapid Tests 1
Barbara J. Smith

Chapter 2: Assessment as Expression of Core Values 11
Rick Wormeli

Chapter 3: Shields Down 17
Barbara J. Smith

Chapter 4: Partnering with Students to Personalize Learning 27
Bena Kallick and Allison Zmuda

Chapter 5: Hiding Places 31
Barbara J. Smith

Chapter 6: It's Not *Just* About Student Engagement 41
Ted Spear

Chapter 7: Time Out 45
Barbara J. Smith

Chapter 8: Time Is a Precious Commodity 55
Emily Walton Doris

Chapter 9: Search Party 59
Barbara J. Smith

Chapter 10: "Don't You Trust Your Students?" 63
Michael Lawrence

Chapter 11: A Show of Force *Barbara J. Smith*	67
Chapter 12: Team Over Faculty *Luke Coles*	77
Chapter 13: Growing Gains *Barbara J. Smith*	83
Chapter 14: Making Professional Learning Visible *Tanisha Nugent Chang*	87
Chapter 15: To Lead or Manage—That Is a Question? *Barbara J. Smith*	91
Chapter 16: Leadership in Designing a New School *John Neretlis*	101
Chapter 17: Political Correctness *Barbara J. Smith*	105
Chapter 18: We Censor Ourselves *Douglas Reeves*	111
Chapter 19: Higher Education *Barbara J. Smith*	113
Chapter 20: Post-Secondary Education: The Presence of Invisible Steps and Stairs *Beverley Freedman*	121
Chapter 21: Five Days in October *Barbara J. Smith*	127
Chapter 22: House of Mirrors *Barbara J. Smith*	135
Chapter 23: Saving Students from a Shattered System *Eldon "Cap" Lee*	143
Chapter 24: The Sausage Machine: Policy Making and School Funding *Barbara J. Smith*	147
Further Discussion: Embrace the Storm	165
References	177

Acknowledgments

I appreciate so much the following experts who wrote chapters for this book, even though I've only met them through emails, LinkedIn, or Zoom calls: Rick Wormeli, Bena Kallick, Allison Zmuda, Ted Spear, Michael Lawrence, Douglas Reeves, Beverley Freedman, and Cap Lee.

Thank you so much for adding your rich voices to this work. I also appreciate the contributions shared by colleagues I have had the pleasure of witnessing firsthand their teaching and learning action, all top-notch educators filled to the brim with passion: Emily Walton Doris, Luke Coles, John Neretlis, and Tanisha Nugent Chang.

Many ideas expressed in *The Gatekeepers* challenge the status quo, so to all those who stepped up to endorse and publish this work, I owe a dept of gratitude. Some messages need to make it to print, and have a light shone on them. Special thanks to the team at Rowman & Littlefield: Tom Koerner, Megan DeLancey, Kira Hall, Jasmine Holman, and Carlie Wall.

After forty years in education, I am so proud that there are so many colleagues and supporters eager to see positive changes in education.

To my family, I owe much thanks, as they did share me with my laptop, too often. They push me to write something everyone would want to read. Thank you, Simon, Sarah, Martin, Molly, and Megan. It's wonderful to have such a strong force backing this Trekkie/educator.

People builders come in all shapes and sizes, and I am particularly blessed with my friends, colleagues, and newfound experts in the field, who all are busy, but made time anyway to read and review this work.

Introduction

GATEKEEPERS BEWARE: A WHOLE NEW WORLD AWAITS

Gatekeepers beware; a whole new world awaits, and transforming school systems is a part of it. The gatekeepers of the industrial school model, established nearly a century ago, need help to change. There should be no shortage of incentives when it comes to moving education from a fixed sunset operation to a more thriving sunrise organization. It is time to storm the clouds of sameness and open the gates to new ways of doing school.

Many believe that the messages in the media sensation, *Star Trek*, influenced a cultural awakening. A source for conversation and lure for visionaries, the science-fiction scripts enticed viewers to think beyond the world as it exists and at the same time examine what things we may take for granted. Gene Roddenberry may have been the founder, but his ideas spawned new generations of writers who continue to keep creativity and goodness at the heart of a purpose, that seems to reach beyond the commercial bottom revenue line.

While the intent of *Star Trek* could be the topic of debate at Trekkie conventions or some cocktail parties, it is a fact that the work is a collaboration that continues after Roddenberry's passing. As former Harvard professor Thomas Richards noted:

> It may have begun as the vision of one man, but viewed in a larger perspective, the series must be seen as a collective achievement, the result of years of collaboration between many different writers, directors, actors, producers, and designers . . . The truth is that it is very hard for a single individual to imagine an entire social world.[1]

A culture cannot shift by the efforts of one person. A school culture cannot grow if stakeholders do not believe the structures in place cannot change.

This book features many ideas that shape new visions for improving education; at the same time, this work identifies and examines how gatekeepers, who cannot see beyond the current conditions in schools, can be barriers to school improvement.

It can take years of collaboration with diverse and innovative mindsets to move stakeholders to storm the gates that limit school change. But it is worth the investment of time and energy to aim beyond the gates schools operate in today.

In education, there are many forces at work that protect schools from the impact of change. Gatekeepers tend to be the people who keep the status quo; they can be anyone within or outside the school structure: government officials, university professors, district leaders, principals, teachers, parents, and even students. They may be part of an elegantly crafted defense system, or they may, in their lackadaisicalness, passively sit on the gate itself.

Many school gatekeepers realize the importance of change, and often purport how others need to do so. Many stakeholders may not be aware of the depth of actions that can fall under the umbrella of gatekeeping. This inquiry will share stories of educators who have run into barriers as well as accounts of risk takers who found ways to navigate around them. Each short chapter will outline a description with examples of gatekeeping and the possibilities for ways educators can open, breach, or remove gates that restrict innovation and engagement.

Gatekeepers are the people whose actions sustain the status quo. They can be resistant to change because of philosophical positions that are often informed by their experiences and unrealistic responsibilities that beseech too many initiatives be addressed at the same time. This examination of gatekeeping focuses on actions that shine a light on fixed positions that are commonplace in many schools. Each chapter examines ways to navigate change considering the restrictions.

In the first chapter, *Rapid Tests*, the industrial hangover of ranking students and schools is addressed in detail. An overemphasis on standardized tests and quantitative metrics accepts the condition that some students can succeed while others may not. Schools that move to mastery learning remove the overengineering and reliance on dated ranking systems.

Chapter 3, *Shields Down*, features what engaging experiences can be like when teachers are permitted to design their own curriculum. When systems lower their shields and remove gatekeeping habits, students can benefit from many quality choices including innovative curriculum, interdisciplinary projects, action research, and the use of engaging resources.

Hiding Places (Chapter 5) reveals where new ideas for improving education can be hidden from view. What books, research, and resources are permitted to inform teacher practice, can limit the options for student and teacher learning. Rather than support a critical thinking culture, gatekeepers will often limit the opportunities to consider alternative perspectives. Innovative ideas can be minimized within jargon-filled excessive text or surveys that do not reach beyond the current practices of schooling.

Chapter 7, *Time Out*, features a deep look at how time constraints limit possibilities for change and improvement in schools. The school calendar, schedule, and minute counting in a school day has become its own science, often taking a dominant position over teaching and learning.

Many hiring practices can use gatekeeping tactics. Chapter 9 focuses on how the educational *Search Party* selects staff. Certain approaches can add or diminish the talent load of an institution. Often many individuals on hiring teams may not be aware that the tools and processes they implement may be flawed. Time dedicated up front to increasing the critical mass of talent can also reduce the overall strain on a system when teachers are hired without the necessary preparation or motivation.

Chapter 11, *A Show of Force*, explores how the tension between individual and collaborative actions can contribute to an accepting or isolating culture, one that removes barriers, while the other keeps them intact. This chapter begins a conversation about the complexity of school cultures and forces where group dynamics, loyalty, polarization, -isms (i.e., sexism, racism . . .), and a sense of belonging can influence how well a staff can function and support, or not, school improvement.

Growing Gains (Chapter 13), unpacks the narrow use of training and professional development (PD) so commonplace in many schools. This chapter addresses the indoctrination of gatekeeping practices in systems designed to avert rather than accept change. The importance of language is examined as well as how to make a vision, mission, and strategic planning more conducive to substantive school improvement.

To Lead or Manage—That Is a Question? (Chapter 15) focuses on the links between training and management and how they can differ considerably from leadership. A leader can facilitate meaningful change with a growth mindset, while a manager tends to focus on polishing the current practices and systems in schools. The job descriptions of those in positions of responsibility in schools and school districts can play a key role in moving school improvement in a forward direction.

Chapter 17, *Political Correctness*, personifies how voices, fearful of change in school communities, can use a serious of cards to put the brakes on projects that steer too far off the traditional school path. Many school leaders will use the "safety card," the "legal card," the "technology card," or the "equity card" to grind innovation to a halt. An innovator will be wise to consider the collateral damage of change and keep one foot on the brakes to ensure that change can be implemented in a productive and meaningful way.

Chapter 19, *Higher Education*, addresses the force of rejection and how it can play a role either directly or indirectly, with an indifference of sustaining the sameness in schools and their operations. The notion that a greater percentage of rejected admission candidates can contribute to the strength of a school is also challenged and earmarked as a conventional gatekeeping practice, as is the "publish or perish" requirement in university channels.

Five Days in October (Chapter 21) features an examination of tweets that present in real time how a number of teachers are feeling like they are drowning in a sea of expectations. Each comment is telling; the voices raise important issues. Educational systems need to respond before it's too late.

The next chapter, *House of Mirrors*, zeroes in on the unwise practice of scaling schools. Trying to replicate an education ignores the uniqueness of the collection of people and how they interact with one another in a school. Given the sheer importance of teachers, students, and school leaders, it is impossible to create real conditions for teaching and learning that can be duplicated in another setting. Schools should not be formulated as visitors to a house of mirrors, framed and bound by the gatekeeping precision of a recipe book.

Chapter 24, *The Sausage Machine: Policy Making and School Funding*, focuses on the worshipping of school policies as fixed positions. Policy should respond to vision, not be the vision in a school. To increase student and teacher engagement, it must support significant change in schools. This chapter challenges the approaches to budget making in many schools and school districts. While plugging in formulas on Excel spreadsheets can reduce workloads, the practice can also limit progress and innovation at the same time. This chapter promotes the coordination and alignment of policy, strategic planning, school improvement, and the financing of schools based on transforming values, much different than a sausage factory.

The final chapter synthesizes the concerns of gatekeeping with a call for educators to *embrace the storm* and open the flood gates of a complex system. The gates need to let more expectations out and invite new initiatives in. There is much time needed for schools to further discuss the implications of fixed practices and the need for meaningful change, the kind that engages the commitment and action of all stakeholders. Possibilities for how to bring about such change are featured as samples and models that should serve as prompts for schools and systems to develop their own unique approaches to support future teaching and learning.

Guest Author Chapters

Between each chapter, twelve guest authors have shared brief accounts of their experiences as they relate to the previous chapter. In this way the reader can experience multiple voices weighing in on gatekeeping and learn firsthand how critical and creative thinkers can stretch the boundaries to make good things happen in schools.

Opening the Floodgates . . .

For over forty years, the University of British Columbia (UBC) has featured a *Storm the Wall* event during midterms to celebrate the soul of the university's character as revealed through academics and extracurricular activities.

Not many people can say they've done a triathlon in their life. Although, if you've ever participated in UBC's Storm the Wall, you're not too far off. As the biggest intramural event in North America, Storm the Wall combines the three essential elements of triathlon with an extra twist: swimming, sprinting, biking, and running—but at the end of the relay race, a 12-foot wall awaits. Teams work together to send each member over the wall—with 1–2 acting as bases and 1–2 reaching down from the top.[2]

Imagine what schools could be like if stakeholders worked together to help each member over the walls that keep school systems stuck in a rut doing the same things year in and year out?

Star Trek created a world much different than the present. According to former Harvard professor Thomas Richards: "Once considered a cult, Star Trek is now part of the vocabulary of modern American culture . . . I think the meaning of the series can best be captured by looking at how it successfully creates a coherent universe."[3] Imagine what coherence could do to improve schools and school systems?

Different from other texts where targeted questions are posed at the end of each chapter, this book presents two "storm the gate" thinking prompts after the introduction when the reader's ship begins at the Departure Level and after the final chapter, when the reader has returned to the Arrival Level. Each task has been designed to make connections with the reader's gatekeeping and gate-scaping stories, inviting readers to engage with the ideas to make them meaningful for a variety of local and global contexts.

Ideally readers will have a chance to think deeply about gatekeeping after reviewing the detailed chapters in between. To honor the courageous pioneers of a creative series that went where "no person has gone before," each chapter concludes with a quote from *Star Trek*, that may stimulate discussion of connections to Roddenberry's iconic work, or not.

The reader is invited to choose their path on this adventure. Reading all or a selection of chapters is up to you. Storming the gate by engaging in the Arrival and Departure level "thinking prompts" are entirely optional. What course of action one takes after this deep dive into the ramifications of gatekeeping is the reader's choice.

Keep in mind that gatekeeping in schools is not only something that happens to stakeholders, but it's also what stakeholders can do to each other, often without realizing it. It's time to storm the gates of our mind and other barriers so we can be free to improve schools.

Storm the Gate Thinking Prompt (Departure Level)

Using a deck of cards, record on the back, fifty-two fixed things that could be difficult to change in schools.

Start by recording a list of ideas on your own; then compare with a partner. You may need to combine pairs in groups to fill the deck.

Then group them into at least three categories (you may create other categories).

- out of my control to change
- somewhat in my control to act on change
- no interest in making change

Discuss what or who might be the gatekeepers of these fixed items.

Imagine that you had an idea you wanted to pitch for the school or district. When you take it to a school leader, this person agrees to think about it and get back to you. A few days later you receive an email outlining why the idea would not be feasible at this time. What might you do next? (Share a real or hypothetical situation.)

Complete this sentence: "I wish I found time to support the _____ initiative that was proposed."

- Explain what contributed to your gatekeeping action.
- Why do you think education needs to have gates or structures in place?

NOTES

1. T. Richards (1997), *The meaning of Star Trek: An excursion into the myth and marvel of the Star Trek universe*, p. 5–6.
2. UBC Recreation, https://recreation.ubc.ca/2019/02/07/what-is-storm-the-wall/.
3. Richards, *The meaning of Star Trek*, p. 2.

Chapter 1

Rapid Tests

Barbara J. Smith

A real estate agent might recommend a school based on a standardized assessment score, but how would this individual know that one school is supposedly better than another? A quick glimpse of a data dashboard may reveal that one school has an overall average on rapid tests that may be higher than others, but does this mean the school is a wise choice? Not at all.

According to Wormeli, "What is fair isn't always equal, and our goal as teachers is to be developmentally appropriate, not one size fits all."[1] Too many schools and school systems place unrealistic demands on teachers and students. He adds, "The inappropriate demand of a lock-step curriculum sequence by age, sharpened by the human need to impose order and schematics on something inherently disorderly and messy to prove accountability"[2] is not preparing young people for the world of college, work, or life.

Wormeli advocates for effective teaching and learning approaches that support differentiation: "Differentiated instruction is doing whatever it takes to ensure that our students can learn well."[3] The number of students requiring varying needs is not addressed in the typical state or provincial school rankings. The assumption is that each school must have an equal distribution of students with distinct special needs. Not so.

Standardized tests do not consider the critical mass of exceptional learners in most school districts. Everyone is tested, with few accommodations provided, if any, in the form of extra time. It appears standardized assessments can bypass the legal requirements as outlined for identified students in their "individual education plan," as if there are no specific assessment regulations as part of their education.

Beyond the unfair inclusion of results from students in special education programming there are two serious concerns when educators trust the results for all students. Kohn points out that: "There are really only two flaws with using tests to assess learning: Right answers often don't reflect real understanding, and wrong answers often don't reflect the absence of understanding."[4]

Altwerger and Strauss suggest that "big corporations" promote standardized tests claiming their interests in controlling the "social order" go beyond the goal of making profits from the sale of textbooks and testing materials.[5] According to Novinger and Compton-Lilly, the textbook industries promote intellectual compliance and "serve particular interests while silencing voices," further arguing, "Although this type of knowledge assessment eliminated the level of corruption, it diminished the role of the teacher and creative approach in students' knowledge assessment."[6]

Rees was concerned that forcing instructors to focus on content that could be measured in standardized tests leads to the avoidance of including analytical material that ultimately can hinder the learning process.[7] The idea of feedback being outsourced to others beyond the classroom, emphasizes the forced separation of assessment and curriculum from teaching and learning. Such action fuels a rudderless direction in education. Health professional, Tasleen Akhar, from Pakistan, shared her concerns about the net effect on the quality of human resources in her country:

> Who else but the teachers are in a position to understand the issues of teaching and learning, to document them and to research and report them. I am not in a position to give an opinion on the state of education in other countries but with an adequate level of confidence can say that education in Pakistan is directionless, teaching learning methods are stuck in the passive transfer of knowledge mode and its objective has been reduced to the passing of exams to get degrees to get jobs. As a result, the quality of human resources is deteriorating from year to year.[8]

It's unfortunate that many school and district leaders ignore the peer-reviewed educational research that does not support dated ranking systems. For systems to thrive, they must describe measures of quality learning in terms of mastery. Does it not make sense that a community, a society, or a nation has a depth of passionate and productive learners, not a skewed proportion of few excellent and exceptional learners? Education is complex, and any attempt to simplify it to a single page dashboard of quantitative results is irresponsible.

If the tools used to rank schools and students are flawed, then how can anyone say that one school is the best? More importantly, how is it that ranking, an industrial hangover from the past century, is still so valued by the public and the education systems that serve them?

An overemphasis on standardized tests and quantitative metrics accepts the condition that some students can succeed while others may not. Schools that move to mastery learning remove the overengineering and reliance on dated ranking systems.

Often ranking systems support the use of "averages," a comparative question often asked by parents or shared by teachers as some arbitrary measure of the middle. Those well above this mean often feel pretty good about such status, but more worrisome is the impact such sharing can have on students below or near the middle of the pack. The goal for all students is to learn and the degree to which the scales deviate learning represents an engineering feat that does little to engage or motivate learners.

Gatekeeping is alive and well when standardized tests use percentages or when classroom rubrics divide the learning into levels of at least three or more that compartmentalize mostly degrees of what students do not know. In the real world, our worth is not reduced to a number, nor does it fit into a quadrant. So much overengineering and attention to categorizing learning can be almost mesmerizing, seducing the implementer into assuming that deviation means value, when it may actually be more about compliance, memorization, and a limited predictor of future success and innovation.

Bloom claims that: "given sufficient time and appropriate types of help, 95% of students . . . can learn a subject up to a high level of mastery."[9] All parents want their children to learn what is being taught, not simply some of it, but all of it. As Guskey noted: "being proficient in not sufficient," Furthermore, he added, "If the grades or marks are criterion-based; that is, based on what students have learned and are able to do rather than students' relative standing among classmates, then teachers have already identified mastery."[10] He claims, "we need to worry less about what label is attached to that level (highest) and more about what we can do to help all students achieve it."[11]

The use of pass-fail, project-based work with clearly defined expectations, standard-based feedback, and tools where the number of parameters is reduced can support better consistency of use, and in turn students could see the value and connection between the curriculum and assessment. They can use it more as a tool for designing and polishing their work, rather than comparing themselves to an arbitrary grade designation.

Traditional report cards have not changed much in the past century. The average of all work in a term gives the student and parent an average gauge of their achievement, which in turn has a detrimental impact on most students who score below a B grade. Heaven forbid, if a school stopped publishing an honor roll!

The emphasis of feedback might be of more value if specific tasks of the work deviates whether the work met expectations with some help (good/apprentice) or met expectations without help (excellent/expert). It should not be about how quickly the material is learned.

Where is the research that reveals that students with C grades or below improve their work after viewing their report cards? This practice does nothing to help student engagement, yet the gatekeeping remains in place because that's what everyone is used to.

Many ideas for improving classroom assessment are presented in the book, *Assessment Tools and Systems: Meaningful Feedback Approaches to Promote Critical and Creative Thinking*. In the following example (Table 1.1), students can use the interactive rubric as a guide for self-assessing their written work, and returning to the same work to upgrade it, if it does not meet at least a B standard (24 or 48 points).

A math portfolio could be much more than a collection of tests. It should include evidence of learning leading up to a test or quiz, and as an application of the learning, ideally using a collaborative approach in designing something with a partner.

So, what would a math portfolio look like? In Table 1.2, a portfolio assessment sample is provided whereby the teacher can assess the learning in the

Table 1.1. Sample Interactive Writing Rubric

Self-Review	2 = excellent level of evidence; 1 = some evidence. NY = not yet	Teacher Review
	Ideas presented in a logical manner (a nice flow)	
	Ideas include solid details	
	Ideas include original creative thought	
	Strong and organized beginning paragraph	
	Captivating starter sentence	
	Strong and organized middle paragraphs	
	Strong and organized ending paragraph	
	Inspiring/memorable ending sentence	
	Use of sophisticated nouns	
	Use of sophisticated verbs	
	Use of words and/or punctuation to transition sentences smoothly	
	Use of a variety of sentence types for emphasis	
	Accurate grammar	
	Accurate spelling	
	Accurate punctuation	
/30 points	Scores (Mastery 48 points or greater)	/30 points

Comments:

B. J. Smith, *Assessment Tools and Systems: Meaningful Feedback Approaches to Promote Critical and Creative Thinking* (Lanham, MD: Rowman & Littlefield, 2023).

Table 1.2 Portfolio Interactive Rubric Feedback Sample

Self-Review	2 = excellent level of evidence; 1 = some evidence; NY = not yet	Teacher Review
	Practice notebook included corrected examples of reducing fractions to lowest common denominators	
	Test revealed precision in reducing fractions to lowest common denominators	
	Practice notebook included corrected examples of multiplying fractions	
	Test revealed precision in multiplying fractions	
	Practice notebook included corrected examples of fraction division	
	Test revealed precision in dividing fractions	
	Practice notebook included corrected examples of adding and subtracting fractions with common denominators	
	Test revealed precision in adding and subtracting simple fractions (with common denominators)	
	Practice notebook included corrected examples of adding fractions with uncommon denominators	
	Test revealed precision in adding complex fractions (with uncommon denominators)	
	Practice notebook included corrected examples of subtracting fractions with uncommon denominators	
	Test revealed precision in subtracting complex fractions (with uncommon denominators)	
	Practice notebook included corrected examples of changing improper to mixed fractions	
	Test revealed precision in changing improper to mixed fractions	
	Practice notebook included corrected examples of changing mixed to improper fractions	
	Test revealed precision in changing mixed to improper fractions.	
	Game design (with partner) for teaching fractions included reducing fractions, changing between mixed and improper fractions and questions (with answers) using each operation	
	Cooperated with partner to design game and use teacher ideas shared in planning talks.	
	Game design was prepared with care (use of ruler, attractive features, easy to read and follow rules)	
	Reflection on teaching fractions through game revealed deep understandings of fractions and use of fraction language	
/40 points	Scores (Mastery 48 points or greater)	/40 points

Comments:

notebook, learning from a test (and re-takes of tests), as well as the learning happening in the preparation and design of a math game on fractions, a game students can use with younger math buddies as an enrichment activity in other classes. The gathering of reflections on math can happen during teacher discussions about the student notebook work, a conference about the test result, the planning of the game design and its implementation with younger students, as well as evidence shared during end of unit reflection (written in prose of point form including diagrams).

Such an assessment tool looks much different than an averaging of test scores or the tracking of photocopied math sheets filled with too many questions, that can dull engagement, precision, and mastery.

In social studies, science, and other forms of coursework, students are often expected to talk about what they know. Without specific direction on what quality talk is, it can be difficult for students to improve on such communications. This sample (Table 1.3) from *Assessment Tools and Systems* provides a tool for use in any subject area. Teachers can add in content expectations to be shared to customize for any discipline. Talking science, math, social studies, English, and leadership contributed to deep learning, reducing the need to repeat the teaching of the same topics year after year.

Table 1.3. Sample Interactive Discussion Rubric

Self - Assessment	2 = excellent discussion habit; 1 = some evidence of good discussion habit; NY = good discussion habit not yet evident	Teacher Assessment
	Responded to questions with careful thought	
	Took notes that record the contribution of others in the discussion	
	Used notes/diagrams made during discussion	
	Asked questions in a whole-class discussion that added to the conversation (no repeat ideas)	
	Waited for silence before contributing to a discussion	
	Linked to others' ideas; responded with names of classmates	
	Expressed ideas in 2–3 sentences	
	Listened with an interested body look	
	Spoke with a respectful tone	
	Encourages others to contribute to discussion	
/20 points	Total Score: /40 points	/20 points

Comments:

Smith, *Assessment Tools and Systems.*

Table 1.4. Sample Interactive Discussion Rubric (using letter grades)

Self-Assessment	A = excellent discussion habit; B = some evidence of good discussion habit; NY = good discussion habit not yet evident	Teacher Assessment
A	Responded to questions with careful thought	A
B	Took notes that record the contribution of others in the discussion	B
B	Used notes/diagrams made during discussion	B
B	Asked questions in a whole-class discussion that added to the conversation (no repeat ideas)	A
A	Waited for silence before making a contribution	A
A	Linked to others' ideas; responded with names of classmates	A
B	Expressed ideas in 2–3 sentences	B
A	Listened with an interested body look	A
A	Spoke with a respectful tone	A
B	Encourages others to contribute to discussion	NY

Comments:

Your question, "What makes you think the main character in the story can be trusted?" brought out some interesting points of view from your discussion group. It was also impressive that you used Tony, Raphael, and Juanita's name throughout your interactions. In your next discussion, be sure to invite participation from the quieter members of the group.

Smith, *Assessment Tools and Systems*.

The same rubric can be reworked with letter designations, which remove the point gathering option. The goal would be for the student and teacher to identify which expectations have been achieved at an A level, which refers to ample and consistent evidence, an excellent demonstration of understanding, a B level, which refers to some evidence, a relatively good level of understanding, and "NY" or "not yet" indicating that the expectations need more work.

Table 1.4 illustrates how in this case there does not need to be an overall grade letter assigned. The teacher conference about the student's participation can focus on how to improve the expectations in the next discussion as well as a clarification where assessment differs. The rubric is not a final score, but a benchmark at a point in time.

Points may seem to be more objective, but using fewer letter grades, and focusing on the degree to which standards have been met, while giving students the opportunity to improve, makes assessment closer to curriculum in that it encompasses teaching and learning as the goal, rather than ranking. The separation of assessment from curriculum could be at the source of much disengagement in schools today.

Such interactive rubrics can be designed by teachers to align their assessment and feedback with the goals of their lessons. Students can also be encouraged to create assessment tools. Interactive rubrics require less reading of excessive prose on the part of students and can serve as a guide to learning and returning to work to improve upon it. Removing the verbiage can open the flood gates enabling more students to get to the point of learning, and not be lost in the weeds; reducing the busy work can help more students move through the gates of learning more freely.

The goal is for more students to succeed, and such tools promote rigor at the same time as mastery. The ranking of students runs counter to the goals of inclusion; after all taxpayers in public institutions and tuition-paying families in independent schools should not be subsidizing an education for mainly the higher-ranking students.

It can take time to move the assessment needle especially given the investment of time gatekeepers have devoted to developing the current tools and systems of standardized operations. Resistance to assessment change must be expected and factored into an overall plan for change.

The quality of education needs to meet the individual needs of each student. The more students in a class, the more challenging it can be for a teacher to meet all needs. Energy needs to be spent on reducing class sizes, rather than exceeding the average on standardized tests if indeed education of the masses matters.

Report cards should not reveal what the curriculum is; they should clarify what the student knows, not what the student knows relative to others in the class. With all that students learn in a term, it should be impossible to list it on a single page report. Twenty-first-century reporting practices should be portfolios filled with evidence of growth and creativity.

Schooling is much more than an aggregate score or an amount of Twitter, Instagram or LinkedIn followers. A school that promotes apprenticeships in a variety of fields such as carpentry, medicine, technology, or law can report on the innovations and inventions that students learn about at novice, apprentice, or expert levels, much more like the world of work. Educating all stakeholders about more progressive models of reporting and documenting learning is needed to address many exclusive patterns of ranking, expected as "standard practice."

So how do you know if one school is better than another? The problem is the question. Pitting schools against one another to "reach for the top" means there will be winners and losers, and given that schooling is for everyone, losing is neither equitable nor acceptable. All stakeholders need to get on with teaching and learning, and put the ranking in its place, the past.

The goals of schooling should have more to do with increasing the critical mass of knowing students who are engaged and passionate about learning, then whether more students have been fooled by questions on a multiple-choice test. To live is to change, but without change, improvement is impossible.

> *"Change is the essential process of all existence."*
>
> –Spock

NOTES

1. R. Wormeli (2018), *Fair isn't always equal: Assessment and grading in the differentiated classroom*, p. 8.

2. Wormeli, *Fair isn't always equal*, p. 9.

3. Wormeli, *Fair isn't always equal*, p. 5.

4. A. Kohn (September 9, 2022), Twitter.

5. B. Altwerger & S. Strauss (2002), The business behind testing, *Language Arts, 79*, pp. 256–63.

6. S. Novinger & C. Compton-Lilly (2005), Telling our stories: Speaking truth to power, *Language Arts, 82*, p. 198.

7. J. Rees (2001), Frederick Taylor in the classroom: Standardized testing and scientific management, *Radical Pedagogy, 3*(2), Retrieved on June 15, 2021, from http://radicalpedagogy.icaap.org/content/issue3_2/rees.html.

8. T. Akhar (September 20, 2022), LinkedIn.

9. B. S. Bloom (1968), Learning for mastery. *Evaluation Comment* (UCLA-CSIEP), *1*(2), p. 4.

10. T. R. Guskey (August 18, 2016), New directions in the development of rubrics, http://tguskey.com/new-direction-in-the-development-of-rubrics/.

11. Guskey, New directions in the development of rubrics.

Chapter 2

Assessment as Expression of Core Values

Rick Wormeli

Assessment, testing, and grading policies are the clearest expressions of one's pedagogical and andragogical, core values. As a result, when one of those policies is questioned, we feel threatened, defaulting into defensiveness, for our basic tenets as educators are on the line.

Ego can be a stubborn thing, of course. It stings when we learn we were not as wise and effective as we thought we were. Everyone succumbs to their inherited narratives from time to time: You know, those narrow lenses through which we see people, teaching, and the larger world that often seduce us with the comfortingly familiar yet take us disturbingly far from our principled beliefs. Hypocrisy worms its way under our skin, and we numb ourselves to its wriggle. Our rallying cry to storm the education castle ebbs, ceding student achievement in the process.

This cannot stand. Here and now, Dylan Thomas,[1] we do not go gentle into that good night; in fact, we rage, rage against the dying of the assessment light! Am I being a little over the top here? No. At times, we must rattle our skeleton and roar our physiology in moral and professional, "WTF?" in order to forge both the courage of conviction and the stamina needed to confront and dismantle what is so deeply entrenched.

As thoughtful professionals, we are the incessant, candid voice for matching teaching practices with sound assessment principles, even to the point of annoying colleagues and the public with the unapologetic theme, and even when it is not politically expedient. We do this each day a student's future is at stake which, indeed, is every single day. There is no rest for the principled, but compellingly, rest is not so urgent, as principled teaching and assessment create their own dynamo.

So, for what in assessment does the Klaxon sound? And in turn, with what new lenses do we see our assessment efforts? Hear two of the calls:

Assessment is not an indictment, nor is it accountability. Question the crowd that justifies testing and any form of assessment by using them to rank schools, "hold students accountable," or to make sure something "counts." This is coercion and forced orthodoxy via embarrassment—not the stuff of successful teaching. These statements are uninformed politicking, not instructionally sound practice; they are school or district/division leadership out of its depth. More importantly, such thinking blunts assessment's powerful learning effect, and then we wonder why our assessment program isn't helping students achieve.

To focus on making something count in a grade's tabulation is an awful way to teach students self-discipline, engagement, or to "hold students accountable." The wiser course is to help students see that our content and skills ***matter*** to them, meaning that the curriculum resonates, and there is hope, interest, and utility in the learning: *Look how this empowers this other thing, Because we spent time on that, we can now do this, You can use this skill to get your voice out there to a right audience, Look how what you built helped our senior citizens connect with other generations . . .*

To help students perceive what matters (counts), we increase the relevancy of course content to students' present culture and future goals. We teach in a developmentally responsive manner rather than a one-size-fits-all, false assumption of uniform instruction as the most preparatory for what's to come, and we facilitate a heck of a lot more agency (voice and choice) in the ways students learn and how they demonstrate that learning.

We also shift the sources of validation for hard work and accomplished learning in our classes from us teachers to students (students' self-monitoring of progress goes a long way here!). We create a ready culture of repeated attempts at demonstrated proficiencies with helpful feedback and the efficacy to act upon that feedback along the way and be assessed anew, instead of one-and-done sequences with no real growth from successive iterations.

In short, assessment is far more a matter of instructional design, than accounting. It's gathering information for students to monitor their learning and using it to light the way forward. In fact, assessments should be listed in the instructional methodology section of our lesson plans. Yes, we can list the criteria for the final levels of proficiency elsewhere in our template, but the biggest use of assessments is in students' formative learning.

Let me finish this segment with a reminder, too, that we need a renewed emphasis on assessment literacy and repertoire in our teachers. So many have a limited sense of what's available to them, what makes for effective assessment design, particularly as a tool of learning not merely documentation, how to analyze student products against evaluative criteria, or how to make feedback based on actionable and student-owned assessment.

Consider: Many of us depend on linguistic skills like talking and writing as the primary avenues for students to express content knowledge, when there are plenty of nonlinguistic methods that can express that knowledge just as clearly and far more accurately, especially for students where the classroom language is not their natural language or for those challenged with learning disabilities.

In addition, a lot of teachers rely on methods associated with extroverts to measure engagement in classroom instruction or demonstrate students' proficiency with content, which disrespects the many strengths and methods of introverts who are absolutely engaged and on top of the course content. Expressing one's proficiency via a method with which one struggles does not create an accurate report of the intended standard or learner outcome. And, how about that large, cut in half, Styrofoam ball with colorful clay topography depicting parts of the cell as the final project in the cytology unit? What evidence of the cytology standards does this provide? It's mostly a test of the parents' capacity to purchase art supplies and the student's skill in recreating an online diagram as a 3D model.

And how about students who understand grade-level content, but cannot read on grade level, yet we demand they read on grade-level text and answer questions about the grade-level content? If we're not assessing reading here, but those other content standards, let's provide a recording of the written text to which they can listen, creating a higher level of comprehension of that content than struggled, silent reading affords, and then we can ask them to answer those questions.

Assessment formats, a family's socioeconomic status, and teacher biases cannot get in the way of accurate expressions of proficiency. Again, we must be vigilant here, dismantling policies and practices that do not align with modern, assessment integrity and purpose.

Assessments themselves are usually not the issue; it's whether the data from them are used punitively or diagnostically. Teachers are fine with local and large-scale assessments if (a) they get the results in timely manner; (b) the results are used to inform teachers and schools, not evaluate them in high stakes judgements; and (c) the results are provided in a way that help teachers improve their classroom instruction.

Continuing with this idea, *Assessment is not for ranking or sorting.* Barbara has made this case well here in her book, but I would add that comparing one student, school, state, or province with another, especially when done without context and based on something as fragile as test scores or reported grades which can vary for a myriad of reasons, or without deep knowledge of what ranking assessments can and cannot report (often missing in real estate offices and local news releases), is deeply flawed. Such ranking invokes massive and unnecessary amounts of time, energy, angst, and unhelpful feelings of superiority or complacency. (We're good, we don't need to remain attentive to things.)

The functional outcome of ranking schools really doesn't change much in classroom instruction and student achievement compared to so many other better uses of time and energy. Unexamined rankings are usually a ball tossed back and forth at neighborhood barbecues or as justification to, "re-arrange the deck chairs," in a half-hearted effort to reform failing schools. The ROI (Return on Investment) is so low, in fact, it's surprising how many would-be education pundits promote it. Ranking's prime effects are often demoralization and a false sense of significant instructional and programming differences among schools in one community, neither of which help education's cause.

We can have assessments that help schools become more effective with their students, of course, but to use these same tests in a manner for which they were not designed and to indicate that one school with a report a few points higher than another school in one or more unexamined categories can better serve students than other schools, and using this to justify higher home prices or a better location? Not even close. Yes, if there was something dire in the nature of a school, such as there were three sexual assaults on the campus last year or most of the staff don't differentiate instruction or grade accurately, it's appropriate to judge the school and choose to live elsewhere, if financially feasible. Truly, though, you can have wonderful teachers, powerful learning, and strong community in low-ranked schools, and ineffective teachers, weaker learning, and even less community in higher ranked schools.

Ultimately, ranking schools provides a misleading sense of measurability, as if we're being objective and credible. Learning and student progression, though, are messy and not easily quantifiable. It's often a matter of three steps forward, two steps back, but still moving in the right direction. We do not worship a uniform timeline and manner of learning thinking they are perfect fits for all students.

And good golly, the standards assigned to grade levels are just that, "assigned." They are our best guesses for the age, but not perfectly suited to everyone at the same moment in time. Many students are ready to move past them while others still struggle—and vice versa. Yet we limit students to a predetermined timeline, and we keep packing in more standards than the normal master schedule allows to be taught. This is flying blind and asking students and their families to bear the burden of it.

We teach in whatever ways individual students learn, not simply to present curriculum and document how students fall short of it on the one arbitrary date we assign to the class. Humans love orderly schematics and simplistic data (pretty graphics, definitive numbers often devoid of interpretation), but both can obscure what's really happening. In their ceaseless promotion, the public is falsely comforted—or afflicted, and teachers and students don't get the real instruction they need for success.

In assessment, let's achieve escape velocity, untying schools from that which tethers them to antiquated practices. Let's do it from a principled foundation, however, including critically examined pedagogy, and with an advocate's heart instead of an adversary's "gotcha." Students and community futures are at stake here: We can minimize hypocrisy, listen to the bell sound, and do this great thing.

NOTE

1. D. Thomas (1952), *Do not go gentle into that good night*, https://poets.org/poem/do-not-go-gentle-good-night.

Chapter 3

Shields Down

Barbara J. Smith

If change is an essential process for all existence, then what stops or limits change can have a serious impact on the sustainability of humanity. When the starship *Enterprise* moved into possible enemy territory, it was commonplace to hear a commander order "shields up" to protect the ship from unknown dangers. What is different can often emit fear of the unknown as a first response.

It makes sense that educational systems that have cemented operating procedures will react by putting "shields up" to change, but progress can only happen when gatekeepers are receptive to new possibilities, as forerunners for school improvement. When the shields are down, there is room for growth and with such exploration room for blunders. Curriculum design is a risk, but without it, what and how we teach cannot improve.

The choice of what expectations are proclaimed as most worthy of learning is influenced by choices educational experts make at some beginning point in a curriculum cycle. Many school systems have become quite masterful at designing, implementing, evaluating, and revising curriculum.

It can be much easier to accept curriculum ideas for revision if their likeness to the present doctrine for teaching and learning is akin to what stakeholders are familiar with. Outlier ideas that can emerge from peer reviewed research or expert practice, can be met by shields that rarely prepare educators for significant change. Shields maintain the status quo in teaching and learning practices. To address meaningful school improvement, the shields must be lowered.

Schools may choose to support one textbook over another based on a fit with the overall curriculum. The investment in systems, such as the *Common Core State Standards* and the tsunami of materials aligned to support it, represent a powerful force of gatekeepers, particularly ruling the parameters of mathematics and English Language Arts (ELA). Publishers have little choice but to develop materials that support a relatively fixed curriculum.

Innovative resources are often shielded from view when they may not match the district, state/provincial, or national curriculum. It makes sense for publishers to follow, rather than lead, to avoid investing in products with limited demand. The more the curriculum does not permit for creativity, the more it functions as a gatekeeping tool.

Indifference can be a form of rejection especially when educators blindly trust what others designate as "the" curriculum. Professionals need room to breathe and fashion curriculum that they believe best suits the needs of all their students. A culture of compliance keeps the shields up and thumbs down on change. The feelings of apathy and disempowerment loom in schools where teachers model for students how not to make waves.

Even when educational systems are built on the rejection premise as the basis for ranking practices, many students and parents accept the offer, succumbing to cognitive dissonance, a learned helplessness echoed by excuses such as "We can't do anything about it anyway."

According to Sheninger, "Excuses are fueled by elements such as fear of change, a desire to protect the status quo, lack of education or knowledge, top-down leadership, micromanagement, and the unwillingness to take risks."[1]

Reliance on the teaching of resilience may be a way of coping with restraints in a school system, but fresh air will be needed to sustain a mindful experience. Accepting new ideas can be a way forward out of the trapped existence of educational sameness. Even though the compelling accounts of project-based learning are supported by curriculum experts, the routine implementation of such authentic approaches are not commonplace in schools. A lack of opportunities for teachers to pilot sustained project work makes it difficult for the integration of subject matter, and the experience of design thinking to take hold.

According to John Spencer:

> On an academic level, students are more engaged and the information sticks. There's often an increase in student achievement. Meanwhile, they learn key skills like project management, collaboration, and communication. True, these projects will prepare students for the creative economy. But more importantly, they empower students for a creative life. Here, they see that making is magic.[2]

He added,

> We know that there's a time crunch in schools. Materials can be scarce. Sometimes you're stuck with a tight curriculum map. But when you, as a

teacher, empower your students with voice and choice, they become the makers who change the world.[3]

Students engage in meaningful inquiry rather than using pre-planned questions. It often involves a shift from the teacher as the director of learning to the teacher as a facilitator.

Spencer defines "design thinking" as a learning experience where students "create a prototype, whether it's a digital work, a physical product, a service, a system, or an event." Students then "highlight what's working and fix what's failing."[4] At this stage,

> they view the revision process as an experiment full of iterations where every mistake takes them closer and closer to success. Then, when it's done, it's ready to launch to an audience. In this launch phase, they send their work to the world.

Then the cycle of learning begins again, "based on the audience feedback."[5]

The myth that project-based learning lacks rigor is at the heart of limited support by many school leaders. Wagner asks: "When is the last time we asked our students to actually think, act and do what real scientists, historians, mathematicians, authors, or entrepreneurs do to address real-world problems?" He added:

> There is a huge myth in project-based learning that the teacher's job is to simply launch a project, and watch while students magically work towards project outcomes. While that is a nice aspiration; it hardly happens that way. The truth is[—]our students still need a teacher. But NOT one who stands and delivers instruction from the front of a classroom.[6]

Moved by the student actions in project-based environments, Wagner describes his observations: "They are always there. Provoking, meddling, catalyzing, instigating, facilitating, and inspiring gently in the background. And letting their students take centre stage."[7] This kind of change is worth fighting for; whatever systematic blockades may be in place, schools need to make project-based opportunities happen for all students.

Gatekeepers will defend the antithesis of project-based learning; that is, teacher-directed instruction whereby students listen and take notes while the teacher shares the sermon of the day. The problem with such a method, is that the gap widens between the students, who have little opportunity to speak or elaborate on their understandings, while the teacher, who models the language of the subject matter excessively, takes up most of the learning time.

What does it look like to teach by not standing in front of a class? Examples of meaningful curriculum are unfortunately rare, but their impact is undeniable. In Tijuana and San Diego, high school students co-designed

"Amistad" an e-zine (digital magazine) that "captured the explorations of teenagers separated by a border yet bonded through journalistic pursuits covering art, food, photo essays, music, and more." According to High Tech High communications:

> They met in person for the first time at the exhibition of the joint publishing project between students at The Gary and Jerri-Ann Jacobs High Tech High (San Diego) and Instituto México Americano Noroeste (Tijuana). The exhibition was the culmination of a day full of classroom visits, tours of the building, and interactions among the teens from the two countries.[8]

High Tech High supported many projects including case studies where: "students gained a cultural understanding of local Chicano, San Diego and Mexican car club histories. This included study of current political events, racism, and *'el arte de los carros'* . . ."[9]

The creating of engaging teaching and learning experiences begins with the blending of informed based practices. Schools and school systems that encourage teachers to become curriculum designers not only trust these key professionals, but also grant them autonomy by enabling them to customize the design of curriculum informed by such deep learning experiences as those espoused by Habits of Mind, and other authentic, purpose-based curriculum.

For instance, the tenets of project-based learning can be strengthened when students have coordinated activities that build and enhance the Habits of Mind. According to Kallick:

> Habits of Mind are dispositions or thinking behaviors that are desirable attributes for learning and living productively in a complex world. This is not a program but a lifelong framework dedicated to growing cognitive, social, and emotional development for all learners. This framework for thinking is as essential now as when it was first introduced over 30 years ago.[10]

She added:

> When we commit to growing the habits both individually and as a community, we become more thoughtful, responsive, and innovative. Over the years during many social, political, scientific, and economic changes, the 16 *Habits of Mind* still stand and the application in practice has grown our thinking.[11]

At an independent boys' school in Toronto, grade 5 students were studying the province of Ontario which included learning about the uniqueness of many communities. To complement their Social Studies program, the students took part in the following inquiry challenge: "If Sterling Hall were to move to another community in Ontario, where do you recommend it re-locate and why?" When they defended their choices, the mayor of one of the selected communities, who was interviewed via the primary source gathering part of the inquiry, came to hear the pitch and add his support to the student who chose his location.

The project-based framework for the inquiry program was designed collaboratively by the teachers and support staff, who all took part as supervisors for this extensive term assignment. Five inquiry actions framed the project: Wonder, Plan, Seek, Analyze, and Defend. The technology director, librarian, special education teachers, classroom teachers, and the VP, academics, each supported a group of six students as they moved through five phases of their *Sterling Has Action Research Kids (Shark)* projects.

Rather than having the school's library, technology, special needs, and classroom teachers implementing separate programs, the integrated efforts helped students have fewer silos to work in, while having more time and individual support to go deeper into their research. The technology director could introduce new software in the context of science or social studies; the librarian could be a designer of curriculum that didn't compete with the assignments of the classroom teacher; and the special education teachers could teach a small group of students that included the identified students integrated in an inclusive setting.

Based on the impact of the *SHARK Program*, a Research & Technology class was developed for high school students at the Jalen Rose Leadership Academy in Detroit and middle school aged students at the William E. Doar, Jr., School for the Performing Arts in Washington, DC. The model transitioned from five actions to six: Explore, Narrow, Gather, Analyze, Generate, and Educate, formulating the *ENGAGE Model for Inquiry*, which was featured as an "exemplary integrated program" in Drake's book, *Creating Standards-Based Integrated Curriculum*.[12]

Looking at the "ENGAGE" model for student action research projects through the lens of Habits of Mind (Table 3.1), it is possible to improve and deepen such a learning experience. When teachers, school academic leaders, and support staff co-design project-based inquiry models and programs of study, increased ownership over the process and initiative can happen. Teachers can do much more than adopt models. When they become makers of models, they can use the habits of mind to adapt and create improved ways of teaching and learning.

School systems that encourage teachers to be curriculum designers see the value of having teacher-researcher role models working directly with students. An empowering culture can turn learning on its head. Students no longer must tolerate memorization but embrace the deeper level thinking that comes from being makers of new knowledge.

Table 3.1. Embedding Habits of Mind Within ENGAGE Inquiry Model

Habits of Mind	ENGAGE Inquiry Model	Habits of Mind that Enhance ENGAGE Inquiry Model
Creating, Imagining, Innovating	Explore	Questioning & posing problems; Thinking flexibly
Listening with understanding and empathy	Narrow	Persisting; Striving for accuracy; Managing impulsivity
Questioning & posing problems	Gather	Listening with understanding and empathy; Persisting; Finding humor; Thinking and communicating with clarity and precision
Gathering data through all senses	Analyze	Persisting; Thinking flexibly; Striving for accuracy; Remaining open to continuous learning; Managing impulsivity; Thinking interdependently
Applying past knowledge to new situations	Generate	Creating, Imagining, Innovating; Questioning and posing problems; Thinking flexibly; Thinking about your thinking; Thinking and communicating with clarity and precision; Taking responsible risks
Persisting	Educate	Listening with understanding and empathy; Finding humor; Taking responsible risks; Remaining open to continuous learning; Responding with wonderment and awe; Thinking interdependently
Thinking flexibly		
Thinking about your thinking		
Finding humor		
Thinking and communicating with clarity and precision		
Taking responsible risks		
Striving for accuracy		
Remaining open to continuous learning		
Responding with wonderment and awe		
Managing impulsivity		
Thinking interdependently		

Often new approaches become institutionalized as educators seek to adopt trusted models. To ensure consistency of the International Baccalaureate, for instance, the curriculum does not permit for much deviation from the designated program. Even though its mission is to develop "inquiring, knowledgeable and caring young people who help to create a better and more peaceful world through education that builds intercultural understanding and respect," it nevertheless must do so within a fixed framework of operation.

It takes a courageous group of stakeholders to deviate from a norm; but given the current status of student and teacher engagement in schools, it is time to do more than adopt existing models. Educators need to be encouraged to adapt and create new models for consideration.

At the Middleburg Community Charter School (MCCS) in Virginia, parents and students were permitted to be co-learners at a newly formed DaVinci-inspired school. The Family Project initiative required families to co-design and co-construct a Family Project based on distinct social studies or science prompts that were shared for primary and older students in this one-of-a kind SK to grade 5 school in Loudon County.

According to Smith: "Rather than build in scattered responses to homework throughout the school year, parents were invited to become co-learners and creators with their children on one project per term."[13] One project required families to create family trees. One family needed a wagon to bring in an actual tree with family members and their stories shared as ornaments. Younger students and families (K to grade 2) worked on making and writing community post cards. She added:

> In another term the older students created their own planets that featured details of physical geography (i.e. rivers, lakes, oceans and topographic details of land masses), history (i.e. governmental systems) and space science (placement in the universe relative to the planets in the solar system). Students and their families also created a 51st state. [14]

Even more impressive were the four evenings of presentations throughout the school year when parents were permitted to be co-learners, shared their experiences with the community:

> Students took one hour to "present" at their booth, while the parents had a chance to view the other creations; then the parents had their chance to "present" at the booth. Rather than the staff doing the work of helping each student put together a conventional "science fair," they were able to observe how students and families applied learning at home.[15]

The parent role does not have to be relegated to the receiving end of a one-way communication conference for less than five minutes, a few times a year. As one parent shared:

> The *DaVinci Model/Curriculum* and MCCS have been a breath of fresh air! As a parent, it's refreshing to be included in my child's education with . . . opportunities to contribute to brainstorming sessions about shaping the future of the school, and to learn alongside my child with project based and integrated learning opportunities as a family.[16]

Even though 95 percent of the parent and student population participated in each of the Leo Nights that featured the Family Projects, the Director of Education was unable to attend these events. When high profile leaders make time to support events that celebrate innovation in learning, it can affirm the actions in a school, and symbolize courageous leadership. Given the only charter school in the district was granted more liberties than the other public schools, there was already an inequitable tension at play. Any endorsement from the highest office could be construed as promoting inequity. It takes courageous leaders to lower their shields to sponsor and promote new ways of doing schooling, even if it means supporting one school at a time.

A shield is a tool that protects one from potential harm. School systems often use shields to keep innovation from making changes in a culture, and while there are changes, such as an overemphasis on school testing, that are harmful, not embracing change is removing the opportunity to freely address school improvement.

> "Without freedom of choice there is no creativity."
>
> —James T. Kirk

NOTES

1. E. C. Sheninger (2016), *Uncommon learning: Creating schools that work for kids*, p.8.
2. J. Spencer (2022), PBL by design—exploring the overlap of project-based learning and design thinking, https://spencerauthor.com/pbl-by-design/.
3. Spencer, PBL by design.
4. Spencer, PBL by design.
5. Spencer, PBL by design.
6. K. Wagner (2022, September 12), LinkedIn.
7. Wagner, LinkedIn.

8. High Tech High (2022), Tijuana and HTH students exhibit co-created magazine, https://www.hightechhigh.org/tijuana-and-hth-students-exhibit-co-created-magazine/.

9. High Tech High (2023), Projects, https://www.hightechhigh.org/student-work/projects/.

10. B. Kallick (2022, September 15), LinkedIn.

11. Kallick, LinkedIn.

12. S. M. Drake (2012), *Creating standards-based integrated curriculum: The common core state standards edition, 3rd edition.*

13. B. J. Smith (2023, in press), *Teacher shortages and the challenge of retention: Practices that make school systems and cultures more attractive and empowering.*

14. Smith, *Teacher shortages and the challenge of retention.*

15. Smith, *Teacher shortages and the challenge of retention.*

16. S. Williams (2022, May 25), Facebook message.

Chapter 4

Partnering with Students to Personalize Learning

Bena Kallick and Allison Zmuda

How do we put our shields down to usher in a system in which curriculum is the property of both the teacher and the student? In consideration of the typical gatekeeping habit that encourages thinking about curriculum as a pre-destined scope and sequence, we suggest opening the portals to invite students into becoming the authors of their own learning. We need to consider how to avoid offering snippets of knowledge and provide time for more longer-term projects that produce real works to build thinking skills and dispositions that powerfully transfer into life skills.

When teachers are given the opportunity to personalize curriculum for and with their students, they become increasingly more creative and generative. This collaborative work defines a personalized culture for learning in which these four attributes as illustrated in Figure 4.1 are valued and cultivated:

- VOICE: Empowerment comes from an environment in which learners recognize the power of their own ideas and recognize the shift that can happen by being exposed to others' ideas. They build confidence that their contributions impact others around them and become better stewards of what they say and how they say it.
- CO-CREATION: The invitation to join others at the design table signifies respect and trust to shape inquiries, approaches, product ideas, and so on. Learners become the actors not merely the recipients of learning assignments, strengthening a collaborative relationship to imagine, strategize, and draft new ideas and actions.
- SOCIAL CONSTRUCTION: There is real power in feeling that you are not alone, a sense of camaraderie when you are working to cause a

change, create a performance, or build a prototype. Social construction occurs as learners seek out information, ideas, and perspectives to guide task development by consulting experts or peers who have intimate knowledge of the topic and using others as a sounding board to work through ideas or roadblocks.

- SELF-DISCOVERY: Learners need to know enough about themselves to be able to make wise decisions as they navigate through the turbulence of a rapidly changing environment. This comes about as learners uncover how they navigate through the challenges they've set for themselves: how they start making sense of a problem or how they generate an idea, how they handle the frustration of not getting it quite right for the umpteenth time, and how they work through revisions or dead ends by analyzing what happened.

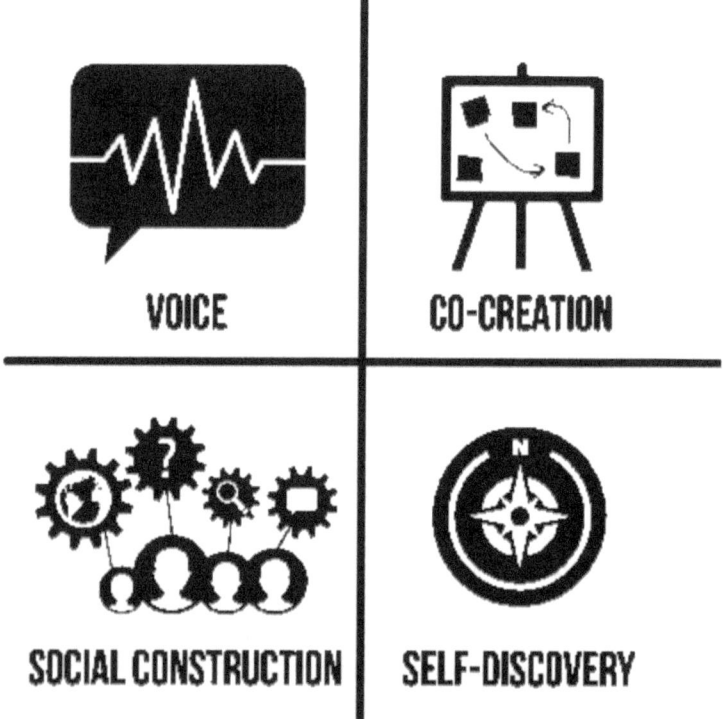

Figure 4.1. Attributes of a Personalized Culture for Learning. *Kallick, B. & Zmuda, A. (2017). Personalized Culture for Learning."https://files.ascd.org/staticfiles/ascd/pdf/siteASCD/publications/books/students-at-the-center-sample-chapters.pdf.*

As we consider these four attributes, new metaphors spring to mind such as a system of inventors, entrepreneurs, discoverers, gardeners. We are committed to creating a culture that is personal, relational, and aspirational. Here are some key patterns we hear as students describe educational settings in which they are most engaged intellectually:

- *When I help define the content—selecting the particular subject of research, the particular biography to read, and the particular play to present.*
- *When I have time to wonder, to work around the edges of the subject matter, and to find a particular direction that interests them.*
- *When I sense the results of my work are not predetermined or fully predictable.*
- *When I believe my teacher learns from my solutions, insights, or information.*
- *When teachers encouraged and respected the different forms of expression and views of the students.*
- *When I have the freedom to create original and public products.*
- *When I can share my expertise with others.*
- *When I had an audience that paid attention to the details and gave a thoughtful response to my work.*
- *When I do something that matters—such as developing a prototype to solve a real problem, participating in a service project.*
- *When my teacher is passionate about what they are teaching and shares their excitement about the ideas associated with the content we are learning.*

The following table provides some prompts for teachers to consider as they aim to develop a more personalized and generative curriculum with students.

Table 4.1. Prompts for a Personalized and Generative Curriculum

Attributes	Reflective Prompts to Consider
VOICE	• In what ways do you invite students to express their thoughts and opinions? • In what ways do you create an environment of safety for students to respectfully disagree with one another (and you)? • In what ways do you give students the opportunity to advocate for a position? • In what ways do you encourage students to raise questions that are skeptical or out of the box?
CO-CREATION	• To what extent do you provide choice for students in WHAT they can pursue (e.g., question, topic, or idea)? • To what extent do you provide choice for students in HOW they can pursue it (e.g., collaboration with peers, consulting outside expertise, seeking out and using resources)? • To what extent do you provide choice to learners for HOW they demonstrate learning (e.g., selection of forms for performance, public vs. private audience)? • To what extent do you provide the opportunity for learners to develop checkpoints and monitor progress in relation to their goal? • To what extent do you create exhibitions for learners that focus on what they learned—about the topic and about themselves?
SOCIAL CONSTRUCTION	• In what ways do you encourage students to seek others to help give their work more meaning? • In what ways do you offer opportunities for students to seek outside of the expertise that is within the classroom? • In what ways do you provide students with the opportunities to test their ideas and see whether they hold up to the scrutiny of others' perspectives?
SELF-DISCOVERY	• In what ways do you provide students with the opportunity to reflect on their learning and how it affects who they are becoming as a learner? • In what ways do you provide the opportunity for students to know more about the ways that they learn best? • In what ways do you provide the opportunity for students to see the growth of their work over time? • To what extent do you create exhibitions for student performances or products that focus on what they learned—about the topic and about themselves?

Through self-discovery, students reflect on their growing capacity to develop ideas, thinking skills and dispositions, and performances, all of which are life skills. Our aim is for learners to consider curriculum as a playground to test out and develop their own aspirations for now and the future.

Chapter 5

Hiding Places

Barbara J. Smith

The over-engineered landscaped views of curriculum are so full of words, it is easy for authentic and engaging learning opportunities to be obscured from view. The need for coaches, academic leaders, and district level coordinators of curriculum to interpret these massive documents is testimony to their futility. Teachers should not need preparation in how to decipher a state or national level curriculum document. With too many expectations, there are too many students who miss the opportunity to gain a deeper understanding of what's essential. Learning hides in the abyss of expectation overload. As noted in *Teacher Shortages and the Challenge of Retention: Practices that Make School Systems and Cultures More Attractive and Empowering*:

> The perspectives of many curriculum developers have become so entrenched with the idea that more evidence is more rigorous, and that more words, pages and prescriptions, especially material housed in elegant prose with glossy packaging, will lead to a utopia of learning. It does appear that after decades of following such assumptions, that students and teachers are not better off for such unproductive efforts.[1]

It is possible to lose meaningful, memorable opportunities when ideas are presented as options for learning. A grade 5 student in Virginia is expected to master eighty-six specific items listed in their Standards of Learning document for English Language Arts. Teachers are expected to make this happen. The *Common Core State Standards* for writing indicate that students in grades 3 through 5 should master thirty multifaceted expectations within a three-year span, with an abundance of repeated work, that makes review of the curriculum, rather than any sense of a fresh experience from year to year.

Some examples of what each item might look like are sprinkled into such curriculum, but they tend to be rare. Unfortunately, the removal of any meaningful context fails to recognize the significance of authentic learning, nor does such a gathering of goals acknowledge the interdependence of learning, expectations, and purpose for learning. Do students not learn to master friendly letters in primary grades or business letters before grade 5?

The jargon that is often used in curriculum documents can also exclude direct access for teachers. For instance, there can be varied interpretations of "Expand and embed ideas by using modifiers, standard coordination, and subordination in complete sentences." A coach or someone outside the classroom is required to decipher, clarify, and help build lessons around the pages and pages of what can be viewed as unrealistic "to do" lists.

Ideas for how to break down such a tall order over a three-year time span are rarely provided; the assumption perhaps that individual states or districts would take it from here. When comparing what grades 3 to 5 students are expected to master, there is some serious overlap. Table 5.1 illustrates the extent of repeated objectives for one cluster of writing standards for Palm Beach County schools in Florida.

In this sample based on standards for the state of Florida, there are three expectations for grade 3, which only include objectives for text types and purposes. There are seven more objectives listed for the "production and distribution of writing," "research to build and present 'knowledge,'" and "range of writing" clusters. To this total in grade 3, are twenty-nine reading standards, eight speaking and listening standards, plus twenty-seven "language" standards, issuing a total of eighty-four English Language Arts expectations. In grade 4, the Florida ELA standards total is seventy-eight and in grade 5, the total number of expectations listed is seventy-seven.

With so many expectations, it can be onerous to make comparisons between grades. It can be overwhelming just to analyze and plan a course of study for seventy-plus standards in one grade.

When there is too much material presented, it is easy to get caught up in the weeds, which can hide clear directions and any sense of what's essential. According to Reeves, "teachers and administrators should collaborate to identify the most important standards—sometimes called 'power standards'—that have the greatest impact on student learning."[2] Smith also acknowledged the need to identify what is essential to learn in schools:

> Beginning with standards, it is the makers of these expectations that have failed to select which objectives are essential and which expectations are secondary or subordinate. Teachers need to be involved in selecting which expectations are essential for all students to master.[3]

Table 5.1. Text Types & Purposes Writing Strands for Palm Beach, Florida

Gr. 3 Writing	Gr. 4 Writing Strand	Gr. 5 Writing Strand
LAFS.3.W.1.1 Write opinion pieces on topics or texts, supporting a point of view with reasons. (CCL2)	LAFS.4.W.1.1 Write opinion pieces on topics or texts, supporting a point of view with reasons and information. (CCL3)	LAFS.5.W.1.1 Write opinion pieces on topics or texts, supporting a point of view with reason and information. (CCL3)
a. Introduce the topic or text they are writing about, state an opinion, and create an organizational structure that lists reasons. b. Provide reasons that support the opinion. c. Use linking words and phrases to connect opinion and reasons. d. Provide a concluding statement or section.	a. Introduce a topic or text clearly, state an opinion, and create an organizational structure in which related ideas are grouped to support the writer's purpose. b. Provide reasons that are supported by facts and details. c. Link opinion and reasons using words and phrases. d. Provide a concluding statement or section related to the opinion presented.	a. Introduce a topic or text clearly, state an opinion, and create an organizational structure in which ideas are logically grouped to support the writer's purpose. b. Provide logically ordered reasons that are supported by facts and details. c. Link opinion and reasons using words, phrases, and clauses. d. Provide a concluding statement or section related to the opinion presented.
LAFS.3.W.1.2 Write informative/explanatory texts to examine a topic and convey ideas and information clearly. (CCL3)	LAFS.4.W.1.2 Write informative/explanatory texts to examine a topic and convey ideas and information clearly. (CCL2)	LAFS.5.W.1.2 Write informative/explanatory texts to examine a topic and convey ideas and information clearly. (CCL2)
a. Introduce a topic and group related information together; include illustrations when useful to aiding comprehension. b. Develop the topic with facts, definitions, and details. c. Use linking words and phrases (e.g., also, another, and, more, but) to connect ideas within categories of information.	a. Introduce a topic clearly and group related information in paragraphs and sections; include formatting (e.g., headings), illustrations, and multimedia when useful to aiding comprehension. b. Develop the topic with facts, definitions, concrete details, quotations, or other information and examples related to the topic. c. Link ideas within categories of information using words and phrases (e.g., another, for example, also, because).	a. Introduce a topic clearly, provide a general observation and focus, and group related information logically; include formatting (e.g., headings), illustrations, and multimedia when useful to aiding comprehension. b. Develop the topic with facts, definitions, concrete details, quotations, or other information and examples related to the topic. c. Link ideas within and across categories of information using words, phrases, and clauses.

d. Provide a concluding statement or section.	d. Use precise language and domain-specific vocabulary to inform about or explain the topic. e. Provide a concluding statement or section related to the information or explanation presented.	d. Use precise language and domain-specific vocabulary to inform about or explain the topic. e. Provide a concluding statement or section related to the information or explanation presented.
LAFS.3.W.1.3 Write narratives to develop real or imagined experiences or events using effective technique, descriptive details, and clear event sequences. (CCL3)	LAFS.4.W.1.3 Write narratives to develop real or imagined experiences or events using effective technique, descriptive details, and clear event sequences. (CCL3)	LAFS.5.W.1.3 Write narratives to develop real or imagined experiences or events using effective technique, descriptive details, and clear event sequences. (CCL3)
a. Establish a situation and introduce a narrator and/or characters; organize an event sequence that unfolds naturally. b. Use dialogue and descriptions of actions, thoughts, and feelings to develop experiences and events or show the response of characters to situations. c. Use temporal words and phrases to signal event order. d. Provide a sense of closure.	a. Orient the reader by establishing a situation and introducing a narrator and/or characters; organize an event sequence that unfolds naturally. b. Use dialogue and description to develop experiences and events or show the responses of characters to situations. c. Use a variety of transitional words and phrases to manage the sequence of events. d. Use concrete words and phrases and sensory details to convey experiences and events precisely. e. Provide a conclusion that follows from the narrated experiences or events.	a. Orient the reader by establishing a situation and introducing a narrator and/or characters; organize an event sequence that unfolds naturally. b. Use narrative techniques, such as dialogue, description, and pacing, to develop experiences and events or show the responses of characters to situations. c. Use a variety of transitional words, phrases, and clauses to manage the sequence of events. d. Use concrete words and phrases and sensory details to convey experiences and events precisely. e. Provide a conclusion that follows from the narrated experiences or events.

Language Arts Florida Standards, Third Grade, https://cdn5-ss14.sharpschool.com/UserFiles/Servers/Server_270532/File/Students%20&%20Parents/Grades%20and%20Graduation/Elementary/LAFS_WIDA_ThirdGrade_Ataglance.pdf; Language Arts Florida Standards, Fourth Grade, https://drive.google.com/file/d/11l6ufKayzYSJoDsgloU61vs07z3n6LFh/view; Language Arts Florida Standards, Fifth Grade, https://cdn5-ss14.sharpschool.com/UserFiles/Servers/Server_270532/File/Students%20&%20Parents/Grades%20and%20Graduation/Elementary/LAFS_WIDA_FifthGrade_Ataglance.pdf.

It could be argued that too much detail can excuse teachers from planning for deep learning and applications to real world scenarios. In many ways, too many expectations can hide clear directions. Curriculum standards can also be stuffed with "edujargon," words and phrases used by educators for educators, making it difficult for other stakeholders to understand the full meaning of expectations. Jargon limits who have access to information. Curricula designed with clarity and transparency can enable more stakeholders to provide more supportive roles for students.

According to Anvi, "elitism through the use of overly complicated words . . . is also a mode of gatekeeping knowledge from the historically marginalized communities, for whom, because of their oppressed status, understanding a language such as English could be a problem."[4] Curriculum materials are often presented to teachers well steeped in jargon. The gap between curriculum development and implementation often widens when teachers perceived that those in "ivory towers," far away from classrooms, are issuing orders that they must follow.

The idea of scaffolding is often used to bridge the gap between what the teacher knows and what the students are going to learn. Furze suggests that "support structures for writing are fine until they become the dominant mode for teaching writing."[5] Teachers should have access to multiple ways of teaching disciplines, and not be tied to one particular process that is formalized by the scaffolding in place. After all, "scaffolds are meant to be torn down."

In the book *Write to Be Read*, Smith and Blecher presented a sample ELA Writing curriculum with far fewer and easier to comprehend words, emphasizing fewer written, but rigorous expectations for each school year (Table 5.2).

Too many standards mixed with educational jargon can act as gatekeepers. Without a clear sense of how all that needs to be learned can happen within the current school structure, the focus can often turn to implementing all that is required, rather than re-organizing expectations for mastery and authentic learning. Fewer expectations do not mean the instruction is less rigorous.

When each standard is taught as a specific lesson objective, teachers have just over two classes to "cover" each objective. The time needed to master the expectations for all students may be much more than two lessons. Educators who view the expectations as a list to get through, do not spend the time needed to synthesize expectations into project-based learning experiences. Many textbooks and resources are developed on a single lesson plan basis that limits the opportunities for making the material meaningful.

The use of black line masters in many resources appear to be time savers, as they can often be aligned with standards, but a graphic organizer, no matter how appealing, for each expectation, perpetuates not only too many disconnected lessons, but also takes away any sense of empowerment teachers may

Table 5.2. Sample ELA Writing Curriculum Areas of Focus

Fiction Reading Themes	Words	Language / Grammar Focus	Sentence Structure & Punctuation	Fiction Poetry	Fiction Focused Writing	Non-Fiction (NF) Poetry	NF Focused Writing
Nursery Rhymes (PK)	identify & record uppercase letters; two-letter words	hard letter sounds	listening and responding to questions	gestures in key words in nursery rhymes	draw & dictate order of events in nursery rhymes	dictate poems about family members	dictate and illustrate stories about family members
Fairy Tales (SK)	upper- & lowercase letters; three-letter words	hard and soft letter sounds	listening to and responding to one-step directions	acrostic poems (fairy tale characters)	dictate own fairy tale . . . "once upon a time . . ."	dictating ABC poems about school	dictate and illustrate stories about people at school
Fables (Gr.1)	simple consonant & vowels; 4-letter simple words	simple action verbs	recording sentences using period and ? mark	rhyming poem about fable	sentences about lessons in fables	shape poems (global city landmarks)	sentences that compare houses in different cities
Folklore (Gr. 2)	complex vowel; compound & blended letter words; alliteration	noun & pronoun use (common, proper)	capital use, titles, point form notes, label maps, short answers	haiku poems; tanka poems	write new endings to folklores.	found poems about nature	create media messages advertising country

Comedy (Gr. 3)	synonyms, similes, puns	adjective use	single paragraph composition, exclamations	limerick poems	character makeover paragraph	looped poems	friendly email letter about to a global e-pal
Adventure/ Mystery (Gr. 4)	antonyms, hyperboles, satire	adverb use	3-paragraph compositions; hyphens, dash, comma use	cinquain poems	write a fictional book review	diamante -comparing past & present	descriptive writing (Middle Ages)
Myths (Gr. 5)	homonyms, onomatopoeia, assonance	phrases, prepositions	5-paragraph compositions, apostrophe use	mythical poem	compare 3 myths	color poems	comparing 3 ancient civilizations
Fantasy (Gr. 6)	metaphor, symbolism, idioms	subject and predicate, adverb clause; conjunctions	article writing novel writing outline	fantasy poems	new worlds for fantasy setting	current event poetry	newspaper article about current event
Science Fiction (Gr. 7)	personification, allusion, flashback	adjective clause	creative writing; speech writing; novel writing draft; colon use	palindrome poems	science fiction writing	technology poetry	STEM & research writing; speech writing

Social Justice (Gr. 8)	irony, allegory, foreshadowing	objects, noun clause	persuasive essay; publish novel; brackets & parentheses	blank verse poems	comparing books by same author	social justice poetry; song writing	business letter writing/letter to editor; abstract
Media, Mentors, Models (Gr. 9–10)	euphemism; analogy; colloquialism;	referencing; quotations; interjections; footnoting	journal writing; cover-ing letter & resume; semi-colon use; slash	Iambic pentameter poems	script writing; film and concert review	poet in the poems	biographical writing; blog writing
World of Work & Life (Gr.11–12)	juxtaposition; oxymoron paradox, motif, soliloquy	text & tools, make a website	documentary writing; debate writing; ellipse	sonnets, ballads, epic poem	comparing authors and messages	writing personal poems	autobiography; annotated bibliography, lit review

Smith & Blecher (2023 in press). *Write to Be Read*. Rowman & Littlefield.

This scope and sequence present the blending of the standards within a learning context.

have to design their own teaching materials. The handbooks filled to the brim with ready-made cookie-cutter lesson plans bound in PDF formats, function as recipe books, when teachers are not encouraged or permitted to modify and adapt ideas to suit the needs of their students.

A teaching professional, as a model of critical and creative thinking, has the capacity not only to analyze the materials shared by their colleagues and their supervisors, but also has a range of reading experience that enables them to see what ideas may not be promoted. Administrators, who may want a more disciplined and compliant culture in a school, may share a breadth of resources that support teacher-directed approaches. Teachers, who have been exposed to more informed educational research, can challenge such expectations and counter with evidence that supports alternative approaches.

When district offices put their stamp of approval on initiatives and mandate specific directives, there is often little room for teachers to negotiate the path; they are expected to row in the same direction, even if the plan goes against the grain of peer-reviewed research. Ideally, district and state/provincial educational leaders would be well versed in grounded pedagogy, but this is not always the case. The gates to school missions and visions can be stormed by change that takes education in a backward direction.

In addition to the overstuffed curriculum, the layers of documentation that states and provinces and districts pass down to individual schools is testimony to the wasted time dedicated to overreporting practices. It could be argued that the busywork of digital entries into complicated databases, leaves little time for teachers to challenge the process or the system itself.

Many media specialists have invested significant time into writing stories about schools, often in response to a tragedy or social injustice. Questions about the learning culture in which students spend over six hours a day cannot be discounted; persistent investigative reporters ask probing questions to try and understand more fully the educative experience. There are some who may fall into the trap of evaluating schools based on standardized test scores, but many are beginning to realize that the testing culture is a deterrent that does little to support all learners in schools.

Finally, where are the satisfaction surveys, and why is it that the raw data is rarely publicized? School leaders who do ask for regular feedback from various stakeholders may view such responses, but rarely does the public see more than an "executive summary." Furthermore, the survey questions are often so general, they rarely lead to supporting innovative directions; rather, their purpose often is centered around gathering evidence to support the current vision and mission of the school. Surveys that function as a conduit for promoting the incredible things schools are doing, do not necessarily inform school improvement.

New ideas for improving education can be hidden from view. The curriculum materials promoted by supervisors and academic leaders do present bias, and in doing so limit the access to diverse possibilities that reach beyond the current practices being implemented in schools today. Curriculum should not be so prescriptive that it does not permit teachers to put their professional stamp on it.

Rather than pages and pages of what and how to teach, districts, states, and provinces should consider the development of power standards and guidelines moving forward. In this way teachers can model critical and creative thinking for their community. Innovation should not be a covert action; it requires courage to make new ideas for improving schools accessible for all.

> "You know the greatest danger facing us is ourselves, and irrational fear of the unknown. There is no such thing as the unknown, only things temporarily hidden, temporarily not understood."
>
> —James T. Kirk

NOTES

1. B. J. Smith (2023, in press), *Teacher shortages and the challenge of retention: Practices that make school systems and cultures more attractive and empowering.*

2. D. B. Reeves (2011), Getting ready for common standards, *American School Board Journal* (March). https://drive.google.com/file/d/1l16ufKayzYSJoDsgIoU61vs07z3n6LFh/view.

3. Smith, *Teacher shortages and the challenge of retention.*

4. Anvi (2021, May 12). How academia & its jargons gatekeep knowledge & uphold class-caste divide, Feminism in India, https://feminisminindia.com/2021/05/12/academia-jargon-gatekeep-knowledge-class-caste-divide/.

5. L. Furze (2022, October), LinkedIn, https://www.linkedin.com/posts/leonfurze_breaking-out-of-teel-activity-6985060758984302594-lWP8/?trk=public_profile_like_view&originalSubdomain=au.

Chapter 6

It's Not *Just* About Student Engagement

Ted Spear

It's not *just* about student engagement; it's about what we think schools should be doing in the first place.

It is now abundantly clear that institutional schooling has more or less lost the plot when it comes to offering something worthwhile and defensible to our youth. This is particularly the case in high schools where any semblance of genuine learning and guided self-discovery have long since given away to a pitiless process of sorting and ranking students according to an effectively meaningless criterion of "student achievement." The teachers who are leaving the profession in droves can be forgiven—and applauded—for refusing to be accomplices to that particular crime.

What is frustrating is that many of the new approaches and innovations offered to defy the status quo—though often worthwhile in their own right—are nonetheless sometimes understood and justified in a way that reinforces, rather than challenges, the very purpose of schools.

Take, for example, the endorsement of project-based learning as a vehicle to enhance "student engagement." If we provide students with more opportunities for project-based learning, they will become more engaged—which, in turn, enables the information to "stick" better, enhances student achievement, and allows students to learn "key skills" (which will prepare them for the "creative economy").

All of these justifications are what I would describe as peripheral or residual side effects—some of which might be difficult to defend as expressions of educational transformation. In offering his account, however, Spencer also includes an important tag to the value of acquiring skills for what he calls the creative economy: "more importantly, they empower students for a creative life." In suggesting that project-based learning might ultimately "empower students for a creative life," Spencer is opening the door to a different—and I think more profound—understanding of the very purpose of schools.

This question of the ultimate justification of project-based learning is important to me because our grades 6 to 9 middle school created a very robust project-based graduation requirement for our grade 9 students. Every year, in mid-June, the grade 9 students each publicly present and defend a "Masterworks" project that they have been working on for the previous eight months. They select a topic of their own choosing and work with an Advisory Committee (one faculty member and two external advisors) to organize their ideas into a fifteen- to twenty-five-page paper that will serve as the foundation of their public presentation. In the presentation itself, they will speak for twenty to thirty minutes and will then take questions: first from their committee and then from the audience at large.

The scope of their self-selected projects and topics is remarkable. There have been fashion shows, dance routines, one-act plays, film and photography exhibits, refurbished motorcycles, poetry and fiction books, self-fashioned boats and surfboards, as well as an encyclopedic investigation of all manner of interests, including:

- Spooky Action at a Distance: Entanglement and Its Applications
- A Contemporary Examination of Multiple Personality Disorder
- Teenage Depression
- Power to the People: A Look at Anarchy and Its Implications in Our Lives
- The Beautiful Game: The Sport That Changes Lives
- The Meaning of Life
- How Are Music and Emotion Connected?
- Remixing the Moonwalk: Teaching the School to Dance Like the King of Pop
- Ernest Shackleton and the Essence of Great Leadership
- The Ethics of Stem Cell Research

Most of these fourteen-year-old students are nervous, some even terrified, about having to stand up and present. But they all manage it—and in many cases, manage it remarkably well—because their faculty advisors have supported them every step of the way, including running them through repeated rehearsals of their presentations. What they eventually figure out is that they are the smartest person in the room regarding the particular project or topic they have chosen to investigate. You can see their confidence increasing as they deal with audience questions. It is a moment in their lives that few of them are likely to forget.

So, on the face of it, this is a worthwhile undertaking with plenty of peripheral and residual benefits. The students learn presentation "skills" they can employ in future situations. They gain the experience of seeing what it looks like to "dig deep" within a particular area of interest. They get to work with adult mentors who share their passion. They get to see that they have the capacity to do something they thought they couldn't do.

And yes, they are "engaged" in the sense that they (sometimes, but not always) enjoy working on their project or topic, they share challenges and insights in their advisory meetings, and they get themselves through a high-stakes public presentation.

But what is the core value or purpose here?

The core value is that project-based opportunities like these are the vehicles through which we invite and enable students to discover and develop their *own* interests and abilities. Spencer understands this when he says that we want to empower students for a creative life. He is suggesting that, when we get right down to it, we want our school system to *set students up* to activate their innermost capacities—i.e., so they can express the very best of who they are. He describes the end goal as a "creative" life, whereas another way to think of this might be to say that we want schools to *set students up* for a life of genuine human fulfilment.

No matter what the phraseology, the point is that the end goal we are striving for is something significantly different—and profoundly more important—than simply serving as a giant accreditation mechanism that sorts and ranks students according to an artificial and externally derived conception of student achievement. Once we have the end goal of empowerment for creativity or human fulfilment firmly and clearly in mind, then the way is clear to re-examine how *all* of our practices, approaches, and innovations might best reinforce and build toward that fundamental end goal.

An example might be helpful. Students completing their Masterworks projects are not graded in any traditional sense. It is more like a "pass/fail" proposition where as long as students complete all the requirements of the project—do the investigation, meet with their Advisory Committee, write the paper, and then publicly present their work—they pass. There is no complicated rubric to dissect each part of the process. At the end of each presentation the Advisory Committee takes a student aside for fifteen minutes to briefly discuss how they thought things went, and to congratulate them on what went particularly well. The Masterworks Coordinator then publicly announces that the student has "met all the requirements of the Masterworks project," and the audience stands up and applauds.

In the twenty-seven years that students have been completing Masterworks projects, no one has ever "failed" for the simple reason that all of the students were fully supported in completing all the requirements of the project. While it is true that some presentations might be regarded as "better" (more compelling?) than others, that is not the point. The point is that each and every student found something to pursue of personal interest, and each and every student pursued and presented this to the best of their ability at the time.

The reason that more project-based investigations make sense—particularly in high school—is not simply because it enhances student engagement. Students can be engaged by playing a well-constructed video game or spending a day at an amusement park. The reason it makes sense is that by carefully and systematically integrating more opportunities for project-based investigations—and by doing a whole host of other things in good faith—we announce and defend a deeper and richer understanding of the ultimate purpose of our schools.

* * *

Ted Spear is the founder of Island Pacific School, and the author of Education Reimagined: The Schools Our Children Need.

Chapter 7

Time Out

Barbara J. Smith

Many educators will admit that time is the most precious commodity in schools. According to Paterson, "if school schedules reflect values and priorities, then we currently value speed, uniformity, quantity over depth, individuality, and quality." Concerned about the "treadmill schedules" that "leave little room for deep learning . . . ," she noted:

> Time is the most controlling structure and the scarcest commodity in schools, and the traditional school schedule is the greatest impediment to educational innovation. Any attempt to redesign the schedule runs up against the intricate constraints of parental custodial expectations, teacher comfort in the known, part-time staff, curriculum mandates, bus schedules, sports schedules, objections from unions, and high-stakes tests. Teachers are held hostage by the sacred timetable, warned that one small change will cause a disastrous cascade.[1]

Teachers need time to plan and time to teach in a way that all students can achieve mastery. Schools would be very different if teachers taught for one-third of the week, planned and took part in professional learning for one-third of the week, and had at least a half hour for lunch with two fifteen-minute wellness breaks throughout each day, for the remaining third portion of their work week. To make such conditions a reality, more teachers would need to be hired.

The four-day work week has often been recommended, but the challenge lies in deciding who could supervise students on the fifth day, if school is no longer operating. Schools are connected to the larger societal system that has adults working five days a week. This means that working parents need schools to provide not only an environment conducive for learning, but one that provides custodial care at the same time.

When schools extended the school day to do more of the same and expect improved results, there was little objection to that trend, but students did miss out on extracurricular programming in and outside the school, and many grew more disengaged with schooling altogether. The research on sleep deprivation is clear that early starts to the day are not supportive of student learning, but parents need to get to work.

If schools reduce the number of months, days of the week, or consider a later start for the day, parents need to find a way to adjust their working schedules. Smith cautioned, "Changes to school time would impact the need for alternative supports to account for the time differential between typical and revised dismissal times. The safety and care of children must be of paramount concern."[2] While safety and learning remain key goals of schooling, the factor of time is a serious force that can support or negate change.

The COVID-19 pandemic led to many more parents working from home, which did impact their productivity, when they were expected to supervise their children learning on-line. The demand for blended work options may or may not create a demand for blended schooling.

Smith warned: "Whether schools implement four-day weeks, early dismissals and/or continue with professional learning days, it is important to look for ways to ensure that students are safe and supervised, especially when many families have fixed 40-hour work weeks."[3]

The need for supervision to some degree of most students remains an issue for "at home" learners. Assuming that a parent can pick up supervisory duties for at least one day per week would not be a wise course of action.

During the pandemic, it probably became evident to many parents viewing the virtual classrooms that what many of their children are learning, and how it is being taught, is not as engaging as it could be. The rapid switch to the digital world, and the disparity of comfort teaching outside the classroom was a factor, but the glimpse into the focus on heavy content and often "busy-work" was often prevalent prior to the pandemic. While engagement does not equal learning, it can be viewed as an interdependent force that moves learners to action socially within the class, and independently with outside related pursuits.

The return to schools after the COVID pandemic has raised concerns about discipline issues in many schools. In the past many behavior issues tended to happen at recess or in situations where students had free time in cafeterias or in hallways. To address the growing numbers of students lined up outside the assistant principal's office after recess, one school established a *Playground Leadership Program* in Mississauga, Canada, where grade 7 students planned and implemented structured games, much like a camp setting for each of the three recesses in the school day.

In the fall and winter, the average number of visitors who had broken the "code of conduct" for the school, was close to 20 usually older students, after each recess. In a school of 350 students, the administration was very busy writing incident reports. Fifteen grade 7 students applied to be playground leaders; many were regular culprits of questionable playground behavior. They took part in weekly lunch hour preparation workshops where they learned new games and shared how things were going with the rest of the leaders who all were scheduled in pairs to lead different recess times throughout the week and then began teaching games to interested younger students.

Students in the primary grades had the option of taking part in the program, which took place over three months, April, May, and June in 1996, over twenty-five years ago. During this time period, the assistant principal had zero incidents to report. This playground leadership program did influence a reduction in poor behavior at this time. Did such a program influence scores on standardized tests? Did the school need to purchase behavioral modification programs to be prepared to react to discipline issues in the school? Did the school need more assistant principals, psychologists, guidance counsellors, or sociologists to address recess concerns?

What is even more striking are the student reflections of the leaders who took part in the program. Not everyone indicated they wanted to return to the role the following school year, but thirteen out of the fifteen did. Their responses gathered in Table 7.1 were telling; the experience seemingly would be memorable, the kind that these young leaders might recall today. In this example, time was wasted when the school administration was reacting, and expecting to react to poor behavior after recess. Time that could have been spent doing other administrative responsibilities or team teaching in classrooms to support learning, was not there when the system did not address the playground problems in a proactive way. Not all students need structure in their free time, but some who had the opportunity to be a leader, and other young students who thrived on structured play, did not have the opportunity to cause harm, as they were channeling their energy in a positive direction.

How can classrooms situate responsibility? What can be done to make learning a more engaging experience? Smith presents a number of alternatives to the industrial model of schooling in *How Much Does a Great School Cost? School Economies and School Values* and in *Teacher Shortages and the Challenge of Retention: Practices that Make School Systems and Cultures More Attractive and Empowering*. Referring to partnering with community resources, Smith noted that schools could re-purpose budgets to support four-day instructional work weeks for teachers, while ensuring that schools remain open for five days a week to accommodate students and families:

Table 7.1. Student Responses from Playground Leadership Program

"You get to play with all the kids."	"It shows me that I could be a good leader."
"It was fun this year." (7) "I like kids." (8) "I did feel left out before, but not anymore because in grade 8 we have a lot of responsibilities to fill our time." "I like playing with little kids." (12) "It is fun playing games with the young ones." "It gives me a chance to make our school better." "I could ask the young kids and the higher grades what THEY want changed." "The little kids look up to me." "I like kids and they look up to the big kids." "I feel if it does not kill you it makes you stronger. Besides it is a great opportunity to give back to the community. Besides I love teaching and instructing." "I prefer to spend recess with my friends." "I think everybody should have a chance to be responsible for a large group of kids." "I like to teach others games so they will have something to do." "I like being outside and working with kids. I think it was a good experience for me since I want to be a camp counsellor when I'm 15 and you need some experience working with kids." "I would like to be a playground leader again because I have leadership qualities. Also valedictorian coming up next year—being in more activities and playground leadership SHOWS like a lot of leadership qualities—so I think that would be a good way." "I like helping them if they had a problem."	"I like going outside." (2) "I like to be a leader." (3) "I'd like to do this again so I would be doing something good to show my mom or dad that I am responsible enough to do things . . . " "I would want to be a playground leader again only if my friends did." "I love playing games and making some games up." "I applied to be a playground leader because I enjoy working and playing with others." "It takes up a lot of time, but it's fun to do, helping with the little kids." (2) "I bring many leadership skills which are needed in life. Everyone needs to be instructed or lead in the right direction or people would not learn." "I don't get along with younger people." "I like teaching kids new games and I love little children." (3) "It was fun to watch the little kids play. They get so hyper and everything." "I did enjoy working with children as it was a new experience. You could teach them sports that they don't know and they could teach you sports that you don't know. So it was kind of a fun experience."; "I learn stuff from them." "You learn new games. I never knew many games before." "I like seeing their expression on their faces when they're excited and everything so I just like cooperating with them—just bonding together." "I think the leaders decrease the fights in school."

"I enjoyed putting the games together to play with the kids."	"Now I know what's expected of me and I'll be ready."
"Maybe the playground leaders could put together all of the games in a book."	"I love working with kids; I would like to have the chance to organize things for kids to do." (2)
"On the last day of school, why don't all the playground leaders come together and play one game with the kids?"	"Maybe grade 6's should have the chance to grow leadership skills being playground leaders."
Importance of enthusiasm (14)	"When we say we have a new game, a whole bunch come running in—or if we have music—or if we have dancing—they get more excited."
"If you're not enthusiastic maybe the kids will think the whole recess will be boring"; "Some people have it more than others"	
"They're pretty cool."	Importance of planning (14)

Schools could work with community agencies to provide special programming for students, as working families may not be able to find additional or affordable childcare. Budgeting to support such programming would need to add significant new line items as there would be real costs associated with internal professional planning and ongoing school improvement activities.[4]

Students in high school senior grades could have one day a week dedicated to internships in local businesses. Students in the middle to upper grades could have elective programming, with or without the option to accumulate micro-credentials in such areas as chess, bridge, leadership, architecture, carpentry, senior's home nursing support, yearbook writing, web-construction, coaching, band, theatre production, refereeing, car repair and building, or a host of nonprofit volunteer charity work. Students in younger grades could work on research projects with the school librarian, special education staff, school administrators, and technology staff.

There are many ways to carve up the thirty-five-hour work week for students and teachers. What teachers require is sustained time, not forty-five minutes, one hour, or a ninety-minute block of time. To prepare for an enriching, engaging, and impressionable learning experience, teachers need more than one day per week to plan and take part in ongoing professional learning. Without such serious changes, stakeholders will need to accept that busywork will continue to exist.

It is possible to expect more, when time to make more memories is systematically applied; after all, with such a focus on accounting for every minute a student is at school, would it not make sense to identify better options for student learning? Reducing the volume of teacher-student interactions could actually improve the quality of the learning experiences, if teachers had time to learn and apply more engaging approaches.

The world of work is so closely associated with traditional timing of schools, it makes it difficult to change seemingly fixed school arrival and departure times. The industrial models of work and school were disrupted during the COVID pandemic, which forced an opening of the gates. The desire, however, to return to normalcy, when schools opened again, can be considered a gatekeeping force driving the system back to what's predictable.

While the opportunity to improve upon what was in place prior to the interruption, was and could be a proactive response, it would require a critical mass of educators with growth mindsets, open to risk new directions for education. How malleable the schedule can be, is a force that can open many possibilities. To provide more time for teacher preparation and growth, the school does not have to literally schedule a day off each week for teachers. It can be a challenge to imagine how students and teachers could be engaged and function with revised timings to support enhanced preparation (Prep) and professional learning (PL), but the following sample schedule (Table 7.2) illustrates one sample of how it can be done.

Table 7.2. Sample Grade 3 ELA and Social Studies Teacher

	Monday	Tuesday	Wednesday	Thursday	Friday
8:00	Gr. 3 Homeroom				
8:30AM	Prep/PL	Prep/PL	Prep/PL	ELA	Prep/PL
9:30AM	Prep/PL	Prep/PL	Prep/PL	Prep/PL	Prep/PL
10:15AM	Recess Supervision	Recess Supervision	Recess Supervision	Recess Supervision	Recess Supervision
10:30AM	Prep/PL	Prep/PL	Prep/PL	Prep/PL	Prep/PL
11:00AM	Wellness Break	Wellness Break	Wellness Break	Wellness Break	Wellness Break
11:30AM	Lunch				
12:15PM	ELA	ELA	ELA	Gr. 3 Team Planning with ELA mentor	ELA
1:00PM	ELA	ELA	ELA	Gr. 3 Team Teaching with ELA Mentor	ELA
1:45PM	Recess Supervision	Recess Supervision	Recess Supervision	Recess Supervision	Recess Supervision
2:00PM	Social Studies	ELA	Social Studies	ELA	Social Studies
3:00PM	Dismissal Supervision	Dismissal Supervision	Dismissal Supervision	Dismissal Supervision	Dismissal Supervision

In this sample, the grade 3 teacher has a weekly scheduled team planning and team-teaching time with a mentor teacher, who provides customized professional learning in the context of the teacher's classroom. In this model, the mentor teachers support teachers but also have their own instructional time with their own classroom. Different from coaches or academic leaders who tend to be completely removed from the classroom, students can still have access to the teacher-leaders as their teachers.

Increasing the number of teacher mentors increases the critical mass of teacher-leaders in a school who ultimately support school improvement and growth. Rather than having a few academic coaches, who do not teach students directly, a school can make room for more mentors who also teach part-time. A school crawling with leaders is not a bad thing.

So, what could a high school schedule look like with more time for preparation and professional learning? Table 7.3 illustrates how a grade 9 ELA teacher, responsible for three different classes of students in one semester can be afforded sufficient time needed for preparation and ongoing professional learning.

Some administrators might look at this schedule and interpret it as a part-time position, but this is precisely the mindset that needs adjusting. To prepare for engaging classes, there should be equal time, if not more to prepare for them.

Table 7.3. Sample Grade 9 & 10 ELA Teacher

	Monday	Tuesday	Wednesday	Thursday	Friday
8:00	Gr. 10 Homeroom/Advisory				
8:30AM	Prep/PL	Prep/PL	Prep/PL	Team Planning with ELA mentor	Prep/PL
9:30AM	Prep/PL	Prep/PL	Prep/PL	Prep/PL	Prep/PL
10:30AM	Prep/PL	Prep/PL	Prep/PL	Prep/PL	Prep/PL
11:30AM	Wellness Break	Wellness Break	Wellness Break	Wellness Break	Wellness Break
12:30AM	Lunch				
12:15PM	ELA10a	ELA10a	ELA10a	ELA10a	Gr.10a Team Teaching with ELA Mentor
1:00PM	ELA10b	ELA10b	ELA10b	ELA10b	ELA10b
2:00PM	ELA9a	ELA9a	ELA9a	ELA9a	ELA9a
3:00PM	Dismissal	Dismissal	Dismissal	Dismissal	Dismissal

Preparation involves building specific classroom experiences as well as developing one's teaching capacities. Time is required for teachers to research new approaches, engage in reflection of teaching and learning, and conduct professional practices such as action research. Paterson claimed that:

> Countries with higher-performing students give teachers more planning time. Teachers in Shanghai have much more planning time than Australian and US teachers. Planning and collaboration time is critical to teacher job satisfaction and we should make it a priority, a big rock that we put in first.[5]

The schedule needs to support both teachers and students. Often the need for equity takes precedence when it comes to timetabling decisions. The overengineering of schedules to ensure that each student receives the same exact instructional time in each class can be viewed as misspent energy, if the time to prepare for such classes is not sufficient. Notably absent from both sample schedules is the artificial labelling of days as numbers (i.e., Day 1, Day 2, Day 3 . . .). Keeping the days of the week as understood universal Monday through Friday, appeals to the value of authenticity; schools are a part of the real world, not separate from it.

It is also popular for schedules to alternate mornings and afternoon classes so teachers can spread out and have equal access to students when they are supposedly more lucid in the mornings. If teachers had more time to plan and prep for engaging classes, it is doubtful that the time would impact engagement. After all many students are highly focused and involved in extra-curricular activities, not tired at the end of the afternoon.

The length of classroom time is also a challenge especially in school systems trying to cram everything in at the same time. Looking at curriculum as chunks that can be accumulated over the course of semesters and multiyear options can be the key that can open the gates to more informed practices and deeper learning.

In Finland students do not study more than four subjects at one time. They are not rushed as many of their classes are ninety minutes in length.[6] Paterson suggested that schools consider adapting Steiner's model of a "deep learning period" where "students focus on a single subject for at least two hours, is another way of shaking up the traditional school day."[7] Recognizing the uniqueness of every schooled situation, she added:

> . . . there is no optimal class length. The best length of a class period will be different depending on the age of the students, the culture, the number of students, and the experience of the teacher. How teachers use the time they are allocated is more important than the length of the lesson. It is not about how long we teach for but how well we teach with the time we have.[8]

The number of classes and expectations with each class is also a factor to consider in school improvement. Even when educators use block scheduling to split the number of classes, so students have four classes one day and a different set of classes the next day, students are still overwhelmed with the overall expectations of seven or eight subjects in a school year. Teachers would never teach so many different subjects; yet everyone expects students to handle the grit of the system.

The educators who may be satisfied with the overprogramming of young people need a time out, a time to reflect and see that the industrial model of scheduling is not working. If it is not working for all students, it is not working. It's time for the Mad Hatter to let Alice out of the rabbit hole and pause the implantation of these structures that seem to be causing more harm than good.

Paterson shared examples of Australian schools taking innovative initiatives with scheduling to support student learning:

> At St. Luke's Catholic College high school students can opt for a supervised study session at 8:30 am three mornings a week, or they can sleep in and start at 10 am—a decision guided by research into sleep and teenage brains. Sir Joseph Banks High restructured timetables to allow senior students half days. Trinity Grammar School has a fortnightly lesson-free day for Grade 12. At Element College, families are able to choose when they take their 12 weeks of holidays per year, without any disruption to their child's learning or anyone else's learning.[9]

In a century that is being defined by flexibility in time, we no longer need to be held hostage by sacred school timetables.

If we value deep learning and human connection, then this should be explicitly built into the school schedule. Cutting back on sitting, listening, and repetition will result in more engaged, thoughtful, and creative learners. According to Bleske, "we are married to a system that has not been properly re-evaluated for 21st century capabilities and capacities."[10] He added,

> The system's scheduling fails on every possible level . . . So much time is spent in transition that very little is accomplished before there is a demand to move on. If the goal is maximum content conveyed, then the system works marginally well, in that students are pretty much bombarded with detail throughout their school day. However, that breadth of content comes at the cost of depth of understanding. The fractured nature of the work, the short amount of time provided, and the speed of change all undermine learning beyond the superficial. It's shocking, really, that students learn as much as they do.[11]

The arrangement of time in schools can benefit some stakeholders more than others. Educators have much to do to explore and examine how time structures can benefit more the needs of all stakeholders.

"Logic clearly dictates that the needs of the many outweigh the needs of the few."

—Spock

NOTES

1. C. Paterson (2022), Timetable absurdity, Getting Smart, https://www.gettingsmart.com/2022/09/12/timetable-absurdity/.
2. B. J. Smith (2023, in press), *Teacher shortages and the challenge of retention: Practices that make school systems and cultures more attractive and empowering.*
3. Smith, *Teacher shortages and the challenge of retention.*
4. Smith, *Teacher shortages and the challenge of retention.*
5. Paterson, Timetable absurdity.
6. Paterson, Timetable absurdity.
7. Paterson, Timetable absurdity.
8. Paterson, Timetable absurdity.
9. Paterson, Timetable absurdity.
10. B. Bleske (2019), The absurd structure of high school, GEN, https://gen.medium.com/the-insane-structure-of-high-school-762fea58fe62.
11. Bleske, The absurd structure of high school.

Chapter 8

Time Is a Precious Commodity

Emily Walton Doris

Time is a precious commodity. With the major responsibilities of school gatekeepers, it is understandable the constraints that are felt in utilizing the time in a day, month, and school year efficiently. In reading the following, I encourage you to frame your perspective through a different lens of efficiency; a lens that sees experiential learning, not as an alternative that takes away from instructional classroom time, but as a vessel of valuable learning time.

The first time I heard the term "medication vacation," I was an assistant director at an overnight summer camp. During registration day, a very distraught mother shared with me that she had taken her son off his ADHD medication for the first time. While she wanted to give him a break from daily doses, she was concerned about the potential side effects on his mood and behavior. I kept a very close eye on that camper over the ten-day session and was thrilled to watch him play, make friends, get dirty, laugh, learn, and have a successful week without his medication.

I do not know if that child was re-medicated on his return to the classroom, but my suspicions are not optimistic for the alternative, as the demands of traditional school life are quite different from summer camp. The reality of being medicated daily to conform to classroom expectations is all too real for many students.

How have we arrived at this place, where students are medicated out of essentially acting like a child? Rather than looking to the system that has perpetuated these expectations and forced difficult parental decisions, the common route is changing the child. I worry about the long-term effects and lessons this holds for our students. There are alternative solutions such as outdoor learning, which host mental, physical, and emotional benefits for students.[1] Fitting the outdoors into a daily school schedule is an option for administrators and educators willing to manage the risks of experiential education, situated outside the fixed brick walls of traditional schooling. For students to reap the rewards of a full education, one that embraces the natural world, the way we parcel time in school needs to change.

Administrators play a key role in access to outdoor experiential learning. A study conducted by Oberle et al. to investigate the obstacles Canadian teachers faced in implementing outdoor education found many of the perceived barriers pointing to the administrative levels of support. Gatekeeping is reinforced when there is limited, if any, school policy support, professional development, and workshop offerings, nor funding for supplies, and finding time in the daily schedule.[2] Without administrative support, teachers struggle to offer quality *Outdoor and Experiential Education* (OEE), regardless of understanding its deep benefits for students.

I have been very fortunate to work for administrators that recognize and value the benefits of outdoor experiential education. When given the freedom to flex my students' schedules to adapt to their daily needs, instructional time is far more productive and efficient. Take, for example, the rambunctious class of grade 2's whom I taught during the pandemic. They were so keen to learn, alas after sitting and listening for two hours, one snack, and fifteen minutes of recess, they were hardly ready to listen when I showed up for class. The children were not the problem, and as our class was at the same time every day, creative solutions were needed.

I decided to begin most classes outside with an active engagement activity. The lesson remained outside, utilizing the natural elements as prompts, making use of the calming environment or we made use of the space to spread out and work. When we did go inside for a portion of the lesson, the students were far more engaged and focused than on the days we did not start outside with active engagement. I did not consider the time taken outside as a loss of learning time. Students were progressing appropriately and the behavioral incidents in the classroom were reduced. Such a simple example of implementing outdoor experiential learning for students was possible with administrative support.

On a different scale, *Forest Schools* provide a creative option of a full day of outdoor learning. Often sought by parents, desperate for alternatives to the traditional classroom, these natural schooling contexts are becoming more prevalent. Many families and school systems are becoming more aware of the value of such once weekly absences from conventional schooling to attend a school outdoors. Creative time solutions, supported by all stakeholders, can benefit all students.

There is so much opportunity within OEE to offer multiple ways of knowing as well as promote understanding and empathy amongst its participants and in their relationships with the land. Combined with the benefits for students and the many ways for connecting the curriculum, I wonder how administrators will challenge the traditional thoughts of time in a daily school schedule to open access to outdoor experiential learning for their students?

NOTES

1. R. Louv (2005), *Last child in the woods: Saving our children from nature-deficit disorder*, 1st edition.

2. E. Oberle, M. Zeni, F. Munday, and M. Brussoni (2021), Support factors and barriers for outdoor learning in elementary schools: A systemic perspective, *American Journal of Health Education*, *52*(5), pp. 251–65, https://doi.org/10.1080/19325037.2021.1955232.

Chapter 9

Search Party

Barbara J. Smith

Schools need employees who are engaged and passionate about what they do. Matching people to fit college programs can be limited by the number of spaces in specific areas making it necessary for individuals to determine a process for selecting successful candidates. The number of applicants for courses like medicine and law can be challenging for decision-makers. There seems to be higher demands for health and legal services, now especially in the shadow of COVID-19, and given there are more people who want to become doctors and lawyers, the system should consider how to increase the number of spaces available.

The current filters designed to select candidates should not be fixed based on set standards developed in a different era. There are many immigrants who without the reciprocal authority to practice their trades or professions, cannot contribute to society in the best way possible. More doctors and nurses are needed, but the gatekeeping requirements and standards are not allowing many experts to step in and provide support. Furthermore, the number of applicants rejected in many fields, including medicine, continue to be high.

Some schools construct profiles that serve as filters to narrow the applicants to those most "suitable." Increasing access to higher education is possible, when gatekeepers consider alternative ways for offering programming to more students. Reducing the supply will increase the demand, and as such the brand of being a doctor, for instance, remains more exclusive, more important. To those in such a profession, it adds more stress on the system as fewer people are there to support the overall health needs in many communities.

Access to more apprenticeships and easier access for reciprocal acceptance of qualifications should allow for various professionals to contribute in productive ways. The filters designed for an industrial society must be flexible to meet the needs of our current society. Tests in a foreign language need to be revised, so as not to exclude but permit better access for people educated from foreign universities. Deliberate connections to global colleges can aid in the process of ensuring that qualifications are reputable.

The most common excuse for the use of tests like the SSAT or ACT or other school admission tests is making fair decisions about who can enter an institution or course of study (LSAT, MCAT, GMAT . . .). The over-reliance on test-taking to qualify individuals into programs of study needs to be examined in light of what can be provided by interviews with candidates and interviews with their references. It seems like many decisions are defaulted to a test score and this is such a narrow slice of evidence of learning and motivation.

More people with an education background could be added to college admission teams to review portfolios and interview candidates to find the right mix of people, rather than the right "fit" of people. After all there is academic strength in diversity, which should include a blend of race, religion, culture, zip codes, interest, and academic diversity; after all the grades students achieve on a standardized tests or report cards are never a true predictor of future success or passion. Gatekeepers need to be reminded of the limitations of relying on ranking metrics as absolute measures of achievement.

To prepare for many higher education experiences, school districts particularly in the United States start the machines as early as grade 3, and continue the testing each year. Book publishers add to this context of deviation, by promoting leveled books complete with software and easy to apply tests for grouping students. Some people believe that individuals who have a bank of facts at their fingertips would make the best teachers. Such a narrow understanding of the capacity of teachers misses the mark on many levels. Kohn claimed:

> This should be obvious, but judging by the claims of education traditionalists, it may bear repeating: Successful contestants on Jeopardy! may also happen to be highly intelligent, but we can't assume that's true just because they've managed to memorize a lot of information.[1]

Many hiring practices also use gatekeeping tactics. Staff selection approaches can add or diminish the *talent load* of an institution. Often many individuals on hiring teams may not be aware that the tools and processes they implement may be flawed. Time dedicated up front to increase the critical mass of talent can also reduce the overall strain on a system when teachers are hired without the necessary preparation or motivation.

It could be argued that limiting the number of pages in a résumé reduces the opportunities for those rich in experience, the kind that spill over into a second or third page. School leaders eager to increase the critical mass of exceptional educators will want to know more about the individuals applying for positions. Portfolios in digital or print form can display images, letters, and plans that give decision-makers a more robust account of what the candidate brings to the table.

Other gatekeeping practices include the outsourcing of reference checks to clerical staff or reducing interviews to a thirty-minute time frame. It makes more sense to invest more time in the upfront selection process than to deal with the aftermath of a poor decision. Some people use the excuse that all reference interviews are glowing, but this is not the case if one asks solid questions. For instance, there is much you can discover when someone shares that a candidate "helped" with an event, rather than "organized" the event.

Does the reference letter or interview indicate that they would hire the candidate? Does the referee describe specific examples of how the teacher supported others, communicated with parents, and demonstrated initiative? No one should assume that reference and reference letters do not provide insight into the candidate; what is included and not included can be very telling. A detailed job description highlighting flexibility, the need for candidates to show initiative, and a desire for continuous growth can be important in setting the ongoing professional learning stage.

To have a seat at the table in education, teachers can apply for opportunities to rise through the ranks to become school principals, superintendents, or the directors of educations in a jurisdiction. They can also apply for district consultant, state, provincial, or national roles, or take on teacher educator roles at faculties and colleges of education. Some can aspire to become deans of education, consultants, educational writers, or designers of laboratory schools. There is no shortage of avenues for promotion.

Such positions of responsibility can carry more weight when it comes to the strategic design of a school system. These school leaders can follow the present path of education, or they can be proactive in building a path that moves beyond the industrial ranking model.

Who are selected to be in such roles and how they are selected can be limited by gatekeeping practices that support exclusive criteria. For instance, in Ontario, Canada, curriculum leaders must be fluent in two official languages to apply for government positions. Teacher educators, new to the field, must have an extensive publication record and be viewed by the culture as fitting into the research focus of the senior members of the community. There does not seem to be much room for diversity of ideas, nor initiative to change the present path of education.

In the United States, the business of authorizing credentials is a colossal business that takes the rigor of thinking and decision-making out of the hands of employers. Regulations that do not accept teachers from other states or countries are narrowing the sphere for operation and limiting the talent load in a jurisdiction.

Affording temporary status or recommending further study for highly qualified professionals should not have to be so onerous. Given the present teacher shortage conditions, it is timely to challenge the depth of bureaucracy that handcuffs the gates to education globally. The lack of access to diverse ideas alone should be cause for concern when policies isolate what happens inside a system from outside influences that could influence positive change.

Trustees, for instance, in Michigan charter schools, cannot reside in other states. A co-founder of the Jalen Rose Leadership Academy dedicated years of his life to support the opening of this high school, yet this accomplished business man, who lives in Tennessee, was denied the opportunity to be a member of the Board of Directors.

To improve education, school leaders from all sectors must be brave enough to embrace change. It's not enough to adapt to a system and prepare future teachers to operate in a dysfunctional ranking reality. School leaders, together with teachers, parents, and students need to identify gatekeeping practices and remove such barriers to school improvement. Education systems that can access talent can build engaging school cultures.

"Engage."

—Captain Jean-Luc Picard

NOTE

1. A. Kohn (2022, September 27), Twitter.

Chapter 10

"Don't You Trust Your Students?"

Michael Lawrence

Gatekeepers. The term itself is a new one for me, but the people it refers to are well known to me. Five or six years ago, I had the pleasure of visiting Finland and spending time in their schools, sitting in on classes and interacting with teachers, and teacher-educators from Finnish universities.

As a teacher of some thirty years myself, it was transformative to say the least. I recall sitting outside a classroom where I had been told to wait for the teacher to arrive. After twenty minutes, he did arrive and I was surprised to find that the room I had been sitting outside of was not empty but contained a class of twenty or so students about fourteen or fifteen years of age. They had quietly been working away on their history assignments before the teachers arrived.

I have seen university-level classes commence work without a teacher present, but not with this age group. I know from PISA test results that Finland is considered to be a couple of years ahead of Australian students. One teacher who taught in both countries put the gap in teaching practice at thirty to forty years! Beyond the perception of apparent gaps, I started to understand that Finnish educators had recruited the best help imaginable in their pursuit of educational success: the students.

While the rest of us were still teaching to the tests, standardizing the curriculum, increasing teaching time and homework, and generally depersonalizing education in every way imaginable, the Finns were doing the exact opposite. And, in doing so, they were achieving greater success on the very criteria that they placed minimal value on, a standardized test. My immediate response was, "Why isn't everybody trying to recreate these methods?"

In any other industry, if you fail to keep up with best practices, then you will quickly find yourself losing customers and (eventually) going out of business. Back home, responses to my tales of Finnish education varied from astonished (and astonished that we weren't trying to do it here) from those who had been there themselves or had taken the time to investigate it, to complete dismissal with a short excuse which varied from "too expensive," to "different society," and many others in between.

While writing the book *Testing 3,2,1: What Australian Education Can Learn from Finland*, I had a detailed look into the reasons behind the Finnish success and the reasons behind other countries' reluctance to follow. It certainly wasn't cost, as the Finns were spending less per student than my own country. One of the keys to Finnish success is the autonomy given to the teaching profession. It is seen in the same light as law or medicine, and as competitive as these to get into. Teachers are encouraged to learn best practice, and then try to improve on it. They are trusted to develop the curriculum from the brief government document into something tailored for their students, as they see fit.

Government and parents respect and trust teachers and rarely, if ever, criticize them. This is why teaching is seen as such an attractive career choice.

Finnish teachers can explain the neuroscience and the research behind every aspect of their practice. They quizzed me on my practice, and why I continued to use it even though it was clearly not bringing success. I began to see that this respect for teachers and education created a profession which was attractive to the best and the personalization of the students' education meant that they had ownership over their studies. I now refuse to criticize teachers, as I understand the damage it can do.

Rather than being "engaged students," they were "inspired students"; students who completed an assignment, not because they wanted the marks, but because they wanted to complete the assignment. When we standardize education for the purposes of comparing and ranking students, we make it about our purposes, not the students. And students quickly come to understand this.

The classroom that I assumed was empty and contained students who were working on their assignments, not the teacher's or the school's assignments. When Finland runs less class time than elsewhere, the quality of that class time is the important thing. When they have almost no homework, this doesn't mean that students are not choosing to work on their assignments at home.

Neuroscience tells us that the brain is not suited to learning when it is in a stressed state. Think about how blocks of time seem to go missing immediately after or even during a stressful event. Finland ensures that students are comfortable and safe at school, that they want to be there. As one student who was on exchange from the USA put it, "Finnish teenagers are still rebellious, but school is not one of the things they rebel against."[1]

Neuroscience also tells us that we learn far more effectively when we have breaks every forty-five minutes or so. Finnish teachers were surprised to find that schools outside of their country were still using up to 100-minute blocks with no scheduled break. A five-minute snack in the classroom does not fit the bill! Gatekeepers seem to be afraid that any loosening of the chains on the gates will see students run amok, like hard core criminals in a prison breakout.

The Finnish educator will simply ask, "Don't you trust your students?" Perhaps we don't trust our students. Perhaps a decade plus at school, having everything they do controlled, restricted, and monitored, has left them with no self-control at all. Perhaps they are incapable of handling any responsibility or making an important decision.

These gatekeepers are ironically often the first people to justify their actions by suggesting that these students will need discipline and responsible judgement in the real world. Meanwhile the Finnish child has been walking to and from school, making decisions about their learning, dressing themselves, and by midway through their school years, coming and going from the school in the same way a university student does.

* * *

Michael Lawrence, author, and English Teacher at St. Ignatius, in Geelong, Victoria, Australia

NOTE

1. M. Lawrence (2020), *Testing 3, 2, 1: What Australian education can learn from Finland.*

Chapter 11

A Show of Force

Barbara J. Smith

When all stakeholders in a school interact, there can be a dynamic interplay of forces. The interface between individual and collaborative action in schools can be experienced at many levels. When students, teachers, parents, school leaders, and district-level administrators interact with one another there is a dynamic tension that impacts a school. Some interfaces can be a force for good in terms of moving a school culture toward positive change, while other interactions can be forces that lock out possibilities for school improvement.

FORCES IN THE CLASSROOM

Students are often held accountable for their learning as individuals, yet often work collaboratively with other students or with the teacher to demonstrate their understanding. The real world is often a social space, so learning with others can be an authentic experience. Vygotsky's constructivist theory[1] suggests that learning requires a social context, but he also addressed the notion that learning moves between the individual and social condition.

To behave like a scientist, one can benefit from interactions with a scientist, but students need individual time to reflect and create using the habits of scientists, separate from the social collection of classroom scientists. For safety and supervisory reasons, there is less opportunity for the individual shaping of thinking.

So, when and how can students deepen their understanding beyond the social context of a classroom? The simple response might be to tack on reflective activities at the end of the day as homework, but the value of added work after a day's work at school is already highly questionable. According to Alfie Kohn, author of *The Homework Myth*:

I've heard from countless people across the country about the frustration they feel over homework. Parents who watch a torrent of busywork spill out of their children's backpacks wish they could help teachers understand how the cons overwhelmingly outweigh the pros. And teachers who have long harbored doubts about the value of homework feel pressured by those parents who mistakenly believe that a lack of afterschool assignments reflects an insufficient commitment to academic achievement. Such parents seem to reason that as long as their kids have lots of stuff to do every night, never mind what it is, then learning must be taking place.[2]

Does this mean that the school day should be shortened, to permit for individual reflection and creativity? Ideally yes, but the tension arises when students cannot be cared for when working parents are not home to supervise them.

Perhaps there are spaces in schools, like libraries, laboratories, or studios that can support more individual work? Would more budding artists, poets, singers, software designers, dancers, writers, and more emerge if they could explore their experiences in less socially vulnerable spaces? Reading, for instance, is not a social activity, and even though DEAR (Drop Everything And Read) advocates fully believe that reading in a social environment motivates students to read, it is doubtful there is evidence to support such a claim.

To move from a novice through apprentice (the social domain) to an expert level of understanding, students need to be able to work with others and then without help on their own. Designing schools for both social and individual learning is a complex challenge, as it would require some re-thinking and re-purposing of the physical plant, as well as new ways of coordinating school staffing. The more traditional schoolhouses are built, based on formulas to house more and more students, the more pervasive the gatekeeping of ineffective learning conditions.

It would also be an assumption that collaborative conditions for learning in classrooms have all been implemented in the most rigorous and productive ways. Often group work is chosen with three or more participants, but it is more difficult to articulate understandings during shared "air time." Paired work may take longer for teachers to assess, but the opportunity for each partner to talk is enhanced greatly. Projects tend be assigned to larger groups but when a pair works together there tends to be much more negotiating and sharing of ideas.

Knight et al. claim that when students explain their answers and discuss them with a peer, they can fill knowledge gaps with new knowledge.[3] Tullis and Goldstone suggested that: "dyads have more information processing resources than individuals, so they can solve more complex problems" and "dyads may foster greater motivation than individuals." He added, "dyads may stimulate the creation of new, abstract representations of knowledge, above and beyond what one would expect from the level of abstraction created by individuals."[4]

Peer teaching, where older students teach younger students, is a powerful learning experience that puts "teaching," with adult guidance, as a learning approach in the hands of students. Schools that promote learning buddies for reading, writing, math, or other subject areas recognize the inherent value of making time for such potent practices. Tullis and Goldstone suggest that peer instruction leverages the benefits of self-explanation and "goes beyond them by involving what might be called 'other-explanation' processes - processes recruited not just when explaining a situation to oneself but to others."[5]

Many researchers including Priniski and Horne[6] claim that students can explain something better to each other while Brown and Palincsar,[7] Noddings,[8] Vedder,[9] and Vygotsky[10] go further to suggest that students can be more effective than experts at explaining concepts because they make use of familiar terms and can focus more on what might not be understood.

Table 11.1 features a collection of research adapted from Tullis and Gladstone's Literature Review that supports the benefits of social contexts for learning.

Lave and Wenger's theory of *Legitimate Peripheral Participation* (LPP)[11] speaks volumes in support of learning in a social context, namely one where novice learners work side by side with experts to learn and use the tools of experts. When students apprentice with experts they use the language of experts to negotiate meaning, and thus deepen their understandings. Internships provide a powerful medium for LPP, as do programs that feature artists and other experts in school residencies.

The Wisconsin Department of Public Instruction (DPI) described how the *Launch Program* has been instrumental in supporting student careers. Pre-apprenticeship program administrator, Craig Griffie coordinates a project-based learning strand:

> In Griffie's program, a professional from each trade works alongside him to teach students masonry, carpentry, electrical, plumbing, and other skills. A free-standing bathroom rises from the shop floor as each phase of the building process is learned. At the end of the project, the bathroom is taken apart, but students can take their skills with them into registered apprenticeship programs.[12]

Different from most apprenticeship models where students are assigned a mentor, these students grapple with real problems that they can work on in class. As Griffie noted, "And because the Wauwatosa program is certified by the Department of Workforce Development as a pre-apprenticeship program, students get a 500-hour credit toward the 7,000-hour registered apprenticeship program through the North Central States Regional Council of Carpenters."[13]

Table 11.1. Benefits of Social Contexts for Learning

Researchers	Findings re: Benefits of Social Learning
Bearison, Magzamen, & Filardo, 1986b; Bossert, 1988c; Brown & Palincsar, 1989d; Webb & Palincsar, 1996e	" . . . teachers often put students in groups so that they can learn from each other by giving and receiving help, recognizing contradictions between their own and others' perspectives, and constructing new understandings from divergent ideas."
Bargh & Schul, 1980f; Benware & Deci, 1984g; King, 1992h; Yackel, Cobb, & Wood, 1991i	"Giving explanations to a peer may encourage explainers to clarify or reorganize information, recognize and rectify gaps in understandings, and build more elaborate interpretations of knowledge than they would have alone."
Chi, de Leeuw, Chiu, & LaVancher, 1994j; Rittle-Johnson, 2006k; Wong, Lawson, & Keeves, 2002l	"Prompting students to explain why and how problems are solved facilitates conceptual learning more than reading the problem solutions twice without self-explanations."
Bielaczyc, Pirolli, & Brown, 1995m; Chi & Bassock, 1989n; Chi, Bassock, Lewis, Reimann, & Glaser, 1989o; Renkl, Stark, Gruber, & Mandl, 1998p; VanLehn, Jones, & Chi, 1992q; Wong et al., 2002r	"Self-explanations can prompt students to retrieve, integrate, and modify their knowledge with new knowledge; self-explanations can also help students identify gaps in their knowledge."
Aleven & Koedinger, 2002s; Atkinson, Renkl, & Merrill, 2003t; Chi & VanLehn, 2010u; Graesser, McNamara, & VanLehn, 2005v	"detect and correct errors, and facilitate deeper understanding of conceptual knowledge"
Duncan, 2005w; Mazur, 1997x	"Despite wide variations in its implementation, peer instruction consistently benefits student learning. Switching classroom structure from didactic lectures to one centered around peer instruction improves learners' conceptual understanding."
Lasry, Mazur, & Watkins, 2008y	"reduces student attrition in difficult courses."
Porter, Bailey-Lee, & Simon, 2013z	"decreases failure rates."
Lucas, 2009a[a]	"bolsters student engagement"
Beekes, 2006b[b]	"bolsters attitudes to their course"

a. Tullis & Goldstone, Ibid.

b. Bearison, D. J., Magzamen, S., & Filardo, E. K. (1986) "Sociocognitive conflict and cognitive growth in young children." *Merrill-Palmer Quarterly. 32*(1):51–72.

c. Bossert, S. T. (1988). "Cooperative activities in the classroom." *Review of Research in Education*. 15:225–52.

d. Brown & Palincsar, Ibid.

e. Webb, N. M., & Palincsar, A. S. (1996). "Group processes in the classroom." In: Berliner DC, Calfee RC, Eds. *Handbook of educational psychology*. New York: Macmillan Library Reference USA: London: Prentice Hall International, pp. 841–873.

f. Bargh, J. A., & Schul, Y. (1980). "On the cognitive benefit of teaching." *Journal of Educational Psychology*, 72:593–604.

g. Benware, C. A., & Deci, E. L. (1984). "Quality of learning with an active versus passive motivational set." *American Educational Research Journal*. 21:755–765.

h. King, A. (1992). "Facilitating elaborative learning through guided student-generated questioning." *Educational Psychologist*. 27:111–126.

i. Yackel, E., Cobb, P., & Wood. T. (1991). "Small-group interactions as a source of learning opportunities in second-grade mathematics." *Journal for Research in Mathematics Education*. 22:390–408.

j. Chi, M. T. H., de Leeuw, N., Chiu, M. H., & LaVancher, C. (1994). "Eliciting self-explanations improves understanding." *Cognitive Science*. 18:439–477.

k. Rittle-Johnson, B. (2006). "Promoting transfer: Effects of self-explanation and direct instruction." *Child Development*. 77:1–15.

l. Wong, R. M. F., Lawson, M. J. & Keeves, J. (2002). "The effects of self-explanation training on students' problem solving in high school mathematics." *Learning and Instruction*. 12:23.

m. Bielaczyc, K., Pirolli, P., & Brown, A. L. (1995). "Training in self-explanation and self regulation strategies: Investigating the effects of knowledge acquisition activities on problem solving." *Cognition and Instruction*. 13:221–251.

n. Chi, M. T. H., & Bassock, M. (1989). "Learning from examples via self-explanations." In: Resnick LB, editor. *Knowing, learning, and instruction: Essays in honor of Robert Glaser*. Hillsdale: Erlbaum, pp. 251–282.

o. Chi, M. T. H., Bassock, M., Lewis, M., Reimann, P., & Glaser, R. (1989). "Self-explanations: How students study and use examples in learning to solve problems." *Cognitive Science*. 13:145–82.

p. Renkl, A., Stark, R., Gruber, H. & Mandl, H. (1998). "Learning from worked-out examples: The effects of example variability and elicited self-explanations." *Contemporary Educational Psychology*. 23:90–108.

q. VanLehn, K., Jones, R. M., & Chi, M. T. H. (1992). "A model of the self-explanation effect." *Journal of the Learning Sciences*. 2(1):1–59.

r. Wong et al., Ibid.

s. Aleven, V. & Koedinger, K.R. (2002). "An effective metacognitive strategy: Learning by doing and explaining with a computer based cognitive tutor." *Cognitive Science*. 26:147–179.

t. Atkinson, R.K., Renkl, A. & Merrill, M.M. (2003). "Transitioning from studying examples to solving problems: Effects of self-explanation prompts and fading worked-out steps." *Journal of Educational Psychology*. 95:774–783.

u. Chi, M. & VanLehn, K.A. (2010). "Meta-cognitive strategy instruction in intelligent tutoring systems: How, when and why." *Journal of Educational Technology and Society*. 13:25–39.

v. Graesser, A.C., McNamara, D., VanLehn, K. (2005). "Scaffolding deep comprehension strategies through AutoTutor and iSTART." *Educational Psychologist*. 40:225–234.

w. Duncan, D. (2005). *Clickers in the classroom: How to enhance science teaching using classroom response systems*. San Francisco: Pearson/Addison-Wesley; 2005.

x. Mazur E. (1997). *Peer instruction: A user's manual*. Upper Saddle River: Prentice Hall.

y. Lasry, N., Mazur, E., & Watkins, J. (2008). "Peer instruction: From Harvard to the two-year college." *American Journal of Physics*. 76(11):1066–1069.

z. Porter, L., Bailey-Lee, C., & Simon, B. (2013). *SIGCSE '13: Proceedings of the 44th ACM technical symposium on computer science education*. New York: ACM Press, pp. 177–182.

aa. Lucas, A. (2009). "Using peer instruction and i-clickers to enhance student participation in calculus." *Primus*. 19(3):219–231.

bb. Beekes, W. (2006). "The 'millionaire' method for encouraging participation." *Active Learning in Higher Education*. 7:25–36.

Some schools promote apprenticeship opportunities where students in senior grades learn in the workforce with experts. Teachers may try to emulate such experiences in the classrooms, but they simply cannot be an expert in every profession. Students thrive in real contexts that are thwarted often by gates of funding, credit requirements, and school structures. Students should learn in optimal conditions, which should be at the forefront of school improvement plans. Gatekeepers of dated systems must make room for change.

Staff Interfacing

The interaction of a school staff can contribute to a positive school culture, or not. How teachers interact with each other, non-instructional staff, and their supervisors can vary considerably from school to school.

Teachers who are motivated to collaborate with other teachers can have a profound impact on the operations of a school. They may share resources, co-plan the design and implementation of curriculum, or take part as mentors or mentees. Some interactions may involve contributing to strategic planning, reflecting on professional learning activities, or taking part in shared action research. These can be highly effective experiences providing they are not coerced or being disingenuous in their collaborative efforts.

Many schools support teacher collaboration in the form of weekly grade meetings. When ample time is provided teachers can share their plans and resources, and ideally co-create activities together. Such time can also be reserved for discussing specific needs of specific students. Often the librarian, academic leader, technology coordinator, and special education teacher may be present. Often such time is less than an hour, making it difficult to move beyond superficial discussions and planning.

More effective staff meetings can provide a medium for collaborative professional learning, and quality interaction, as well. Rather than the sharing of information, which could be compiled in an email communication, staff meetings should be more productive and engaging. Just as students respond to two-way communication, where their voices can be heard, teachers can also be empowered when they can work with each other and the administration to address positive school change.

The relationship between the administration and the staff is a powerful collaborative force, especially when stakeholders are aware of the range of possibilities for school improvement. Professional learning opportunities have a role to play in providing options for the development of a school vision and the strategic plan that drives ongoing change. When stakeholders do not support change, such fixed positions can have an adverse impact on school growth.

There can be some voices on a school staff that are more forthcoming in their opinions. Others may feel intimidated to rub against the grain of those most vocal and decide to keep their ideas and questions to themselves. While it may seem that a staff speaks with one voice, it is not necessarily so. Regular surveys can provide opportunities for the more introverted voices to share their ideas.

Just as students need time to learn socially and individually, so too does a staff in a learning organization. Without dedicated time for staff members to learn about options for improvement, it is doubtful schools can muster significant change. A productive collaborative force requires that professionals in a school exhibit a growth mindset, open to change.

As much as students need to learn from making mistakes, so too will adults in a school learn from imperfection, as change is not a neat or predictable action. Accepting the messiness of coloring outside the lines is required when staff members commit to school improvement.

Consensus is a process used for decision-making, but collaboration occurs when people come together to co-construct new visions and plans. School leaders are usually charged with the design of strategic plans that highlight the mission at the same time as directing change towards the next vision. Having all stakeholders row in the same direction toward the school vision is what makes a collaboration a positive force in a school.

Staff members can become polarized in their views about the direction a school should take. It can be viewed as a loyalty deficit when change is forced on a staff. School leaders often face the tension between school growth and keeping the status quo. While it is much easier to choose a gentle slope of change, it may not be what's needed to move a school in a new, more productive direction. Nevertheless, the power of the status quo is indeed a powerful gatekeeping force.

When individuals in a school oppose a school vision and strategic plan, they may perceive such directives as gatekeeping actions. Ideally, a school can find a way to adapt a vision to address alternative perspectives.

While new initiatives need time to take hold, it is important to consider reducing the number of years in a strategic plan to perhaps a maximum of three years, so that new directions are possible, reducing the wait time and limiting the apathy that can emerge from powerless perceptions lingering in a workforce. It takes time for staff members to feel comfortable with change—to feel like they belong with the new initiatives that accompany new directions.

What would it look like if staff members could generate their ideas for an ideal school? How much time should staff members have to research informed practices and innovative education programs? How can staff members use action research to share how new approaches can contribute to enhancing a school vision? What role can technology play in supporting school improvement efforts? It would be difficult to discuss the possibilities for change without addressing some of these questions posed to set the tone for constructive change in schools.

George Siemens wrote about "connectivism," which showcases the value of the technology interface:

> Connectivism is a theoretical framework for understanding learning in a digital age. It emphasizes how internet technologies such as web browsers, search engines, wikis, online discussion forums, and social networks contributed to new avenues of learning. Technologies have enabled people to learn and share information across the World Wide Web and among themselves in ways that were not possible before the digital age.[14]

Technology can support learning between teachers and students in many ways. It can also seem like it can save time, but users need to be aware that it can limit autonomy. As Dennis Dill, a former school media specialist and current teacher cautioned:

> Tech has evolved and not in a good way ... in the beginning teachers developed tech usage that fit for them (because Apps were not developed) to now where Apps do everything and teachers do what they tell them to do. We think Apps empower us but they really don't.[15]

There are some schools of thought that see ideal schooling as a face-to-face experience and others who believe education is innovative when it is an on-line experience. While the ideal may fall somewhere in between with blended options, it is important to be clear that technology is a tool, not a solution. Technology may support innovative curriculum and practices, but it is not synonymous with innovation. Critical and creative thinking is what humans can do to evolve and survive, on their own and with others.

"There's another way to survive—mutual trust and help."

—Captain James T. Kirk

NOTES

1. L. S. Vygotsky (1981), The genesis of higher mental functions, in *The concept of activity in Soviet psychology,* ed. J. V. Wertsch, pp. 144–88.

2. A. Kohn (2007), Rethinking homework, https://www.alfiekohn.org/article/rethinking-homework/.

3. J. K. Knight, S. B. Wise, & K. M. Southard (2013), Understanding clicker discussions: Student reasoning and the impact of instructional cues, *CBE-Life Sciences Education* 12, pp. 645–54.

4. J. G. Tullis & R. L. Goldstone (2020), Why does peer instruction benefit student learning?, *Cognitive Research: Principles and Implications* 5, https://www.ncbi.nlm.nih.gov/pmc/articles/PMC7145884/.

5. Tullis & Goldstone, Why does peer instruction benefit student learning?

6. J. H. Priniski & Z. Horne (2019), Crowdsourcing effective educational interventions, in *Proceedings of the 41st annual conference of the cognitive science society*, eds. A. K. Goel, C. Seifert, & C. Freska.

7. A. L. Brown & A. S. Palincsar (1989), Guided, cooperative learning and individual knowledge acquisition, in *Knowing, learning, and instruction: essays in honor of Robert Glaser*, ed. L. B. Resnick, pp. 393–451.

8. N. Noddings (1985), Small groups as a setting for research on mathematical problem solving, in *Teaching and learning mathematical problem solving*, ed. E. A. Silver, pp. 345–360.

9. P. Vedder (1985), *Cooperative learning: A study on processes and effects of cooperation between primary school children.*

10. Vygotsky, The genesis of higher mental fuctions.

11. J. Lave & E. Wenger (1991), Situated learning: Legitimate peripheral participation. https://doi.org/10.1017/CBO9780511815355.

12. DPI (2021, November 30), Program launches students on careers, PDI, https://dpi.wi.gov/news/dpi-connected/program-launches-students-careers.

13. DPI, Program launches students on careers.

14. G. Siemens (2005), *Connectivism: Learning as network creation*, http://www.astd.oeg/LC/2005/1105 _siemens.htm. S. Downes (2005), An introduction to connective knowledge, Stephen's Web.

15. D. Dill (2022, October 13), Twitter.

Chapter 12

Team Over Faculty

Luke Coles

As an assistant and then primary "gatekeeper" of schools over the past two decades, I found my focus shifting from the micro to macro and eventually to that thirty-thousand-foot altitude. Floating up there, looking down at our schools . . . what really *are* we?

In Canada, our education systems are governed provincially, and in the province of Ontario, to be called a school, one needs not much more than a handful of students, a filing cabinet that locks, and an adult to identify as Principal. That's simply to *be* a school.

Readers here are interested in being a certain *kind* of school, and I suggest that to seriously engage and empower students, a school needs identity, and that a school's identity is rooted in the adults who work within it. From both successes and mistakes, I am excited to share how a true school team came into being through repeatable strategies (not all of them planned) that started with recruitment, coursed through retention, and persisted even in turnover.

As principal, I oversaw the rapid growth of a new private (fee-paying) school in an old-growth forest neighborhood of Toronto. In just eight years, full-time enrollment exploded from 25 to 200, and part-time enrollment from 50 to 800 students annually. By year seven, we were generating 4M dollars in annual gross revenue with our group-leading Earnings Before Interest, Taxes, Depreciation, and Amortization (EBIDTA) of 34 percent. Why such growth?

Our families both active and prospective would talk about how our school "felt." Word was spreading fast that we were different . . . that our teachers were smart, youthful (nothing to do with age!), fun, and "nice." It was a calm place to go to school, even a fun place, and in stark contrast to the hit-and-miss experiences at nearby pressure cookers. We knew that we had created an identity, we knew that identity was rooted in our staff and faculty, but even on the inside we weren't always clear on how to describe it.

In exploring what went right, we start with recruitment. In every full-time faculty interview, teacher candidates were asked the same question. Really, we would set them up to shine. "Describe to us, and really paint the picture . . . a class that you taught in the past year or so where it felt JUST right."

Most of our full-time teachers would take a moment, and you'd see a spark in the eyes and a shift in energy. As their story built to the climax of the re-enactment, rocket launch, debate, reaction, comeback, goal, or plot twist, they would lose themselves in their response. Several burst from their seats and there in plain sight was the teacher and passion that students everywhere delight in. They would finish, remind themselves that they were in an interview, and apologize for their exuberance.

Those were our teachers. Their highlights weren't about assessment or course content that they felt most expert in; their highlights were those curated experiences that had ignited their students; experiences those students connected to and will always remember.

Contagious, unbridled energy was a requirement to get in the door, and it was something we could talk about and remind each other of on the tough and thankless days, because we could trust that it was there in all of us. It was a significant bond and shared trait that set a foundation for togetherness.

Occasional mistakes in hiring are inevitable, and some courage is required to ensure the wrong and potentially destructive energy moves on. But for those with that secret sauce, the demand is immediate to challenge, engage, and in so doing, retain them. Several times per year, borrowing from my first principal's lead, I'd ask teachers to sit with me and pause in their work day and life to look at their life and teaching, what had changed, and how they might like to shift.

We built together a tool for measuring both the teaching and beyond-teaching components of "the work." The conversation here wasn't one that felt primarily for the sake of the school, nor was it "judgy" and rating the teacher on any kind of external basis. It was the teacher looking at a series of spectra (where neither extreme feels desirable) and plotting for themselves both where they see themselves now, and where they think they'd most ideally be. Table 12.1 illustrates two Spectra Reviews designed to prompt dialogue about the classroom and professionalism.

Quarterly Spectra reviews would begin with a self-directed update, and we would do these with all of us together in a room, seated in a circle, and able to see one another. It was a reflection done with school and team around us, and there would be very few additions or tweaks externally. This was clearly about more than the teaching, but also the person. It was a practice that was about past, present, and future in our school community. It reminded the teacher that they are cared about here, and it left no doubt about next steps being *here*. It was a consistent, repeated exercise that everyone was going

Table 12.1. Sample Spectra Review Tools

SPECTRA: IN THE CLASSROOM		
On the spectra below, mark an "x" where you believe your ideal 'spot' would be. Then an "O" on where it is today. Use the comment section to document any noteworthy goal, situation, or experience.		
Sterile	YOUR SPACE	Romper Room
Comment:		
Diplomatic Immunity	CURRICULUM MANDATES	Prisoner
Comment:		
Contained/Safe	EXPERIENTIAL/WOW FACTOR	Running Away/Wild
Comment:		
SPECTRA: THE PROFESSIONAL YOU		
On the spectra below, mark an "x" where you believe your ideal 'spot' would be. Then an "O" on where it is today. Use the comment section to document any noteworthy goal, situation, or experience.		
Resistant	STUDENT & SCHOOL LIFE	First to Jump in Blindfolded
Comment:		
Contradiction	LIVING IT	Overdone/Alienating
Comment:		
Consistently Down in the Dumps (Eeyore)	ATTITUDE -/+	Positively Out of Control (Red Bull)
Comment:		

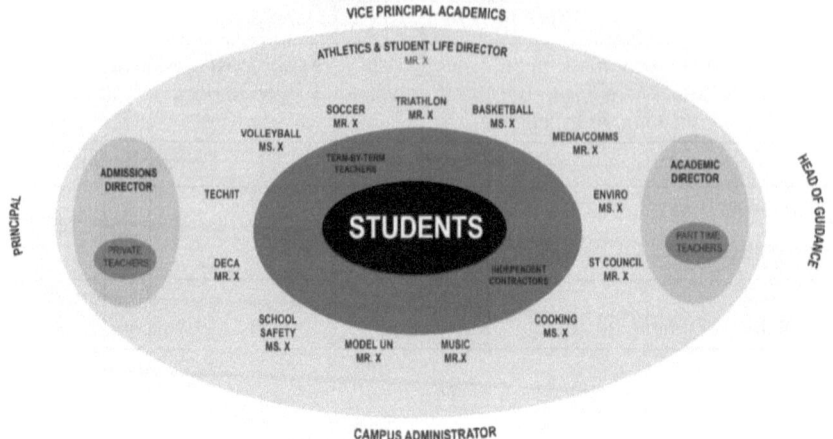

Figure 12.1. Students-as-Core Organization Chart.

through . . . shared, part of being the team, and it made clear in its very design and even existence that people were going to stay with us.

We're not static here; we're moving . . . and your past is here, your now is here, and your foreseeable future is here, so let's just get after it in a solutions-oriented manner and close the gaps between where you are now and where you'd most like to be.

Another tool for the "during" of a teacher's time with us became our Organizational Chart. It began by default as a traditional one; principal and administrators up top, teachers below, students nowhere to be seen. Time passed, though, and we started to clue in as to our developing identity. Our teachers were happy, they liked each other, it was a calm and positive space and place . . . and at the core, it was student-centered.

We were a school not for rules or assessment or even university admissions first and foremost; we were a school for students. With a flipped design, we anticipated the Students-as-Core Organization Chart (Figure 12.1) being well received, but the unanticipated benefit was the transparency of each teacher's role beyond their teaching. By putting this out there to the team, we were saying as administrators that yes, we feel we've done our best to balance what you all are doing as coaches, club leaders, safety leads, and so on.

There were expectations of first-year teachers, and those expectations grew with additional years of seniority. Tasks didn't go to the first to offer; it will always be a select few who volunteer as first to offer and that solves a problem that's in front of you and creates a much bigger problem around the corner. Inequity in out-of-classroom responsibility in schools is a divider and can single-handedly prevent many faculties from becoming teams.

Departures seem an unlikely venue for team building, but here, too, we stumbled upon an opportunity. Being a smaller-scale school that paid teachers less than competitively, our model was one where lengthy tenure was in the 3–6-year range. To encourage more to "stay," our celebration of the departing senior teacher's contributions was also a chance for celebrating and honoring others for their own tenure and contributions. We'd gather, tell stories of what we appreciated most about the departing colleague, and celebrate the team in general. The departing teacher would typically have some impactful things to say about their colleagues and their time with them all, and it often felt like an occasion where others would strengthen their conviction in staying rather than follow suit in the departing.

It was a time for toasters and roasters both to call out their colleague's most memorable moments and attributes, and almost without fail, a time for the identity of the team at large to be commented upon, celebrated, and in that very process, further defined. These were events where newer teachers hardened their commitment to stay, to have impact, and eventually to depart with their own stories and sense of accomplishment just as they were witnessing in their colleague.

The team at its peak was extraordinary. Fifteen to twenty teachers, widely varied in age, attributes, and personality, but deeply together. The positive peer pressure was felt and often commented upon and lifted students emotionally and academically—a high bar of engagement and connection, but with very little competitiveness. Instead, a sense that the impact was precisely in the togetherness.

Curiosity, mentorship, classroom visits, conversations in the staff room that were constructive and encouraging . . . this was a team built on the foundation of the shared traits of being solutions-oriented, passionate about teaching and attunement to youth, and not just a willingness but an insistence to smile, to laugh, and to have fun. Teachers would experience those traits and energies at the outset, throughout, and in the conclusion of their tenure, and these practices fueled the next generation of the team and set the stage for a really special work-and-learning environment for all.

* * *

Previously a teacher and vice principal at The Sterling Hall School, and principal of Blyth Academy, Luke Coles has built a 3-month online experience for young men aged 14–30 through his coaching and consulting company, Thrive, called Structuring for Success. www.thriveto.org.

Chapter 13

Growing Gains

Barbara J. Smith

It may take some time to educate all stakeholders about why the "PD Day" should shift to a Professional Learning "PL" event, but words matter. Professional growth opportunities should be active experiences that involve ongoing learning during designated days and regular weekly scheduled activities where staff members learn on their own and with others. Deliberately absent from this discussion is the notion of training, which is often used synonymously as professional learning for teachers in the school system or candidates in teacher preparation and certification programs.

The term "training" has inherent values that reflect a compliant culture of technicians, not an empowered team of professionals, committed to learning and improving their schools. Just as schools do not function to "train" students, teachers need to be empowered and inspired to participate in professional learning. As Fullan claimed:

> Professional development as a term and as a strategy has run its course. The future of improvement, indeed of the profession itself, depends on a radical shift in how we conceive learning and the conditions under which teachers and students work.[1]

It's time for growing gains, as opposed to growing pains, to be front and center for teachers throughout their schooled experience. Chapter 4 recommends that teachers have at least one hour or more per day dedicated to improving their practice. Rather than developing disconnected skills and taking part in one-size-fits-all workshops, teachers need ongoing customized professional learning experiences, and collective experiences that are linked directly to the schools' mission and vision.

Words can imply a culture that is either compliant or empowered. The nature of professional learning can be challenging for school leaders who want to control the agenda of what and how teachers should behave. Concerned about emphasis on student testing and the collateral impact on teachers, Sheninger noted:

> Newly implemented evaluation systems and the proliferation of new-age standardized assessments have invoked fear among educators like never before . . . this has now led to a monotonous cycle of instruction with the sole purpose of preparing students for the standardized tests that now determine job security for educators and administrators alike.[2]

The use of such scores to define or partially appraise a teacher's worth is the most unfair action, yet, there are some school districts that use such scores in the formulation of teacher percentage ratings. Such unfounded and ungrounded practices need to be called out and shut down.

Often teachers are presented with a single view of research. For instance, many administrators accept "THE" research that concludes that class size doesn't matter. Such a stance ignores curriculum pedagogy that supports the Vygotskian premise of constructivism and co-constructivism. Professional learning should not be about what is done to teachers; for maximum impact, it should be more about what is done with teachers, not simply in the informing stages of exploring new ideas, but in the implementing phases of innovative practices.

Traditional coaching roles involve observations and conversations, whereas more action-oriented experiences involve co-planning and co-teaching with teachers and mentors working side by side in the contexts of real classrooms with real students. Smith claimed that an apprenticeship culture "is often facilitated by deliberate mentorship programs. Typically, seasoned teachers are selected and asked by school leaders to provide support for new teachers to the profession. Effective mentorship programs provide additional preparation time for mentoring activities."[3] Smith shared her experiences in a Washington, DC, elementary school:

> . . . every teaching staff member was either a mentor or a mentee. Mentors were given their own class for half a day, but were free in the other half of the school day to provide support to their mentees. One hour each week the mentor and the mentee met to co-plan a lesson, and the following day, they co-taught the lesson together in the mentee's classroom. The professional conversations, when planning, were grounded in the context of their co-teaching experiences in the classrooms.[4]

Different systems may look at professional learning as an intervention to fix teachers. Such approaches are often focused on indoctrinating other people's values, with the collateral effect of discounting teacher experience. A focus on teacher training rather than professional learning treats educators as technicians.

A comprehensive mentorship program that customizes support, in concert with workshops and collective experiences that support an overall school improvement plan, can have a sustained impact on the growth of an organization. Robust professional learning, according to Smith, "needs to be meaningful, relevant and responsive while grounded in evidence-based practice. Too much and too many disconnected initiatives can do more harm than good."[5] Professional learning can be rewarding and enriching for all involved.

> "This is the twenty-third century. Material needs no longer exist . . . the challenge is to improve yourself to enrich yourself."
>
> —Captain Jean-Luc Picard

NOTES

1. M. Fullan (2007, Summer), Change the terms for teacher learning, Thought Leader, National Staff Development Council. *28*(3), http://michaelfullan.ca/wp-content/uploads/2016/06/13396074650.pdf/.

2. E. C. Sheninger (2016), *Uncommon learning: Creating schools that work for kids*.

3. B. J. Smith (2017), *A charter school principal's story: A view from the inside*.

4. Smith, *A charter school principal's story*.

5. B. J. Smith (2023, in press), *Teacher shortages and the challenge of retention: Practices that make school systems and cultures more attractive and empowering*.

Chapter 14

Making Professional Learning Visible

Tanisha Nugent Chang

Professional development (PD) programs often address different theories of how students and teachers learn; they characterize an essential dynamic in improving teaching and learning.[1] As a teacher for over sixteen years, I have grown to understand that professional learning is for driving success when it is implemented well. Professional learning is a space in which teachers should be challenged to reflect, analyze, question, and learn how to develop themselves as an educator, to improve student learning or as many may say, "close the achievement gap."

Throughout this past decade, it seems like professional learning is becoming less effective. I think the current system falls short when developing teachers to excel at their craft because there is little follow through to help them enhance their craft. The current system can be used to improve teacher performance in their induction phase coming into the profession; however, once they have completed such initial training, there is a lack of follow through to determine what they are continuing to learn during their ongoing professional learning. When the beginning teacher professional learning experience ends, so does the support.

There is also a major disconnect between teachers, administrators, and coaches. The typical focus on mastery of specific teaching skills is not enough. Without examining the impact and desired impact on students, the value of professional development can be limited. School leaders should ensure that professional learning is aligned with teacher appraisal and student learning.

Professional learning needs to be much more than a sales pitch. Often the "trainers" in various workshops tell you about various online platforms to use to improve student learning. Rarely do session leaders address how teachers can improve their teaching styles or how to differentiate a lesson. As a result, teachers continue to struggle with classroom management, content delivery, and differentiation, key hindrances to student success. Educators like the opportunity to have "buy in" and support ideas that will help the teacher to become better.

As a young teacher in a performing arts school, I was given the autonomy to design my own lessons specializing in mathematics. Based on my interest in creating a math curriculum that was vertically progressive from PK to Grade 8, I was asked to take on a newly formed "Dean of Teacher Development" role that included being the "math coordinator," establishing essential skills and understandings in mathematics, as well as mentoring three mathematics teachers on a regular basis.

This mentoring experience required meeting for one hour each week to co-plan a lesson and then co-teach the lesson in the teacher's classroom the next day, followed by cycling in a debrief of the lesson while planning for the next class. This was a very effective method because it allows the teacher to get instant feedback from their lessons; it also built trust and confidence as many mentee teachers went on to become mentors later on in their teaching careers. One mentee went on to become a math leader at a new school.

This leadership role provided customized support and professional learning for the teachers involved, as well as for me. I had the opportunity to witness firsthand how well the vertical alignment of expectations supported students, not only in my own class, in other grades. Different than a coach having a bird's-eye view of teaching, I was a partner in the process, even if only for two hours each week. The dialogue I had with mentees in our planning sessions was enriching for both of us. Being vulnerable as a teacher, with teachers, enabled me to establish trust and in doing so, was accepted as a respected leader, to provide input into my mentees' performance reviews.

Interested in the school's approach to establish fewer more rigorous "power" standards, Alan Ginsburg joined the staff to teach mathematics with me in Grade 8 on a part-time basis. Ginsburg, a world leader in education policy and international math testing, and key author of the *Singapore Math* series, was my mentee, as well. Together we worked collaboratively on an application for a Spencer Foundation Grant focusing on the use of math textbooks as resources to support a curriculum, not be the curriculum. Building a mentoring system of support for teachers contributed to the school gaining close to 10 percent overall gains in mathematics scores in the annual standardized test.

The opportunity to be in a teacher-leader role gave me the confidence to extend my own professional learning, in further graduate studies, Harvard Project Zero,[2] and more recently, taking on leadership opportunities in my current school. During my time at Project Zero, I learned how to step out of my comfort zone and look at how to be a better leader. One of the experiences that stood out for me was the notion of "Making Thinking Visible."[3] Teachers can be more effective when they develop thinking dispositions using three core practices: thinking routines, the documentation of student thinking, and reflective professional practice. This approach helps teachers build thinking routines inside their classroom. Engaging in self-reflecting proved to be a powerful takeaway for me. I was able to make time in my teaching day to incorporate what I learned at Project Zero and support my mentee teachers at the same time.

Unfortunately, for many educators, professional development has become a lecturing tool leaving teachers unfulfilled or ready to implement ideas in their classrooms. If teachers cannot be persuaded that a new approach is valuable and be certain that needed supports will be in place for implementation, teachers are unlikely to adopt them—at least, not without strong accountability pressures.[4] It is particularly important to apply existing theories when challenging teachers' beliefs about, and expectations of, those students who have traditionally underachieved.

If professional learning is implemented well and teachers receive ongoing support after their sessions, then there can be significant outcomes in student performance, teacher growth, and teacher retention. If teachers can be encouraged to take on leadership and co-teaching mentorship roles, they can learn to appreciate and value the broader curriculum and in doing so, have a more comprehensive outlook that can support professional learning as a lifelong teacher experience.

* * *

Tanisha Nugent Chang, Mathematics Teacher, DC Public Schools; Former Dean of Teacher Development, William E. Doar, Jr. School of the Performing Arts

NOTES

1. G. B. Tirozzi & G. Uro (1997), Education reform in the United States: National policy in support of local efforts for school improvement, *American Psychologist, 52*(3), pp. 241–49, https://doi.org/10.1037/0003-066X.52.3.241.

2. Harvard Project Zero. https://pz.harvard.edu/.

3. R. Ritchhart, M. Church, & K. Morrison (2011), *Making thinking visible*.

4. C. E. Coburn (2001), Collective sensemaking about reading: How teachers mediate reading policy in their professional communities, *Educational Evaluation and*

Policy Analysis, 23(2), pp. 145–170, https://doi.org/10.3102/01623737023002145; J. P. Spillane & J. S. Zeuli (1999), Reform and teaching: Exploring patterns of practice in the context of national and state mathematics reforms, *Educational Evaluation and Policy Analysis, 21*(1), pp. 1–27, https://doi.org/10.3102/01623737021001001; H. S. Timperley & G. Phillips (2003), Changing and sustaining teachers' expectations through professional development in literacy, *Teaching and Teacher Education, 19*(6), pp. 627–641.

Chapter 15

To Lead or Manage— That Is a Question?

Barbara J. Smith

To lead is to learn professionally. Leaders focus on the vision in terms of where the school is headed, and managers tend to focus more on keeping the operations running smoothly. Depending on the task at hand, school administrators can be both leaders and managers. A traditional managerial style is less focused on school improvement, whereas a school leader is committed to change that supports the school vision.

Dan Rockwell, writer of the blog "Leadership Freak," suggested: "It's amazing how many people are focused on the past while they complain about the present and worry about the future. Leadership always turns toward the future. You can't lead when you focus on the past."[1] School leaders are challenged to be bold and take risks, but many systems expect compliance and achievement as defined narrowly by high test scores. Sheninger claimed: "A leader's main role is to create an environment that fosters change."[2]

Referring to licensure programs for administrators, Renee Owen suggested that new leaders are expected "to comply with current laws and systems" adding "they aren't training administrators to be revolutionary! So not only are our public school systems not designed for second-order change—which requires changes in beliefs and behaviors—but our leaders are not trained for transformative change."[3] She added:

> In schools, there is a constant striving for *improvement*, but improvement—getting better at what we already do within the systems we already have—will never fundamentally change who we are or how we think. Improvement will never erase inequities. We will continue to get the same results unless we are able to see education in a completely new way.[4]

Leaders are open to seeing education in a new way, whereas managers focus on sustaining the systems already in place.

Lee suggested that:

> Educational leaders still believe that scoring well on a test is an indicator of how students can function in the university, or in life, and the way to achieve this is to sit for a longer time in the classroom until they "get it" . . . And they better do it all at the same time, in the same classroom, talking the same on the same scripted test with the same scripted answers.[5]

What Lee describes is the perspective of school managers dedicated to winning without the insight to see beyond the test in what Lee coins as "the race to emptiness."[6]

Anyone who challenges the system can often limit their potential for promotion within an organization. Improvement is a word often used, but the degree of change can vary significantly. Managers may offer verbal support but may be hesitant to take action. Kyel Easey from Australia suggested that teachers withdraw their investment in the profession when they perceive that the actions of school leaders are not consistent with their words:

> We all have some knowledge that the system is not conducive for best practice and outcomes, so as teachers realise the educational triage of opportunities which are limited by the system we find a way to either burn out or limit our over investment as the verbal value from leaders fails to match the non-verbal value.[7]

When an organization has a critical mass of managers, they can clog up the system with maintenance tasks, leaving little time or room to dialogue about and plan for significant change in an organization. A managerial model supports a top down chain of command, with few educators placed in administrative roles. A leadership model, on the other hand, promotes a more flattened model, where responsibility is situated. Teachers are encouraged to take on teacher-leadership roles, which can include mentoring, action research, and curriculum design.

When more positions are open for teachers to take on leadership roles, they can become more immersed in the language of power that is usually reserved for a few administrators whose voices dominate school decisions. When the gate is removed, and more stakeholders have a say in the design and planning of the school vision, then more people are not only empowered, but more are committed to the school's improvement plan.

According to Sheninger:

It is important not only for teachers to see themselves as leaders, but also for administrators to create the conditions where these teacher leaders can thrive by pushing the envelope through calculated risk taking.[8]

A leadership role should be open to those not afraid to take action to improve things; it should not be a position for simply voicing complaints. Teacher leaders need to have the capacity and commitment to action. Sheninger added:

> Schools need more teacher leaders who are empowered through autonomy to take calculated risks to develop innovative approaches that enable deep learning and higher order thinking without sacrificing accountability.[9]

Creating teacher-leadership roles should involve re-structuring schools. Smith noted:

> School leaders do not benefit from operating in isolation. The more they can surround themselves with talent who can support teachers, the more schools can be ideal places for teaching and learning . . . Flattening the leadership stream to invite more teachers into leadership roles can help decipher and determine school priorities.[10]

The language of power tends to include a collection of obscure language drenched in jargon. As Anvi noted, "Without input or any scaffolding to academic ideas shared from afar, the jargon acts as a power barrier" adding:

> those who can comfortably communicate using the language, are viewed as 'coachable' while those who resist or challenge obscure jargon, are not invited through the gates to future leadership positions. No longer able to deny it, jargons provide a safe space for creating niche "cliques" within academia.[11]

It is important, as Anvi suggests that educational language "talk to and not down on its readers."[12]

Language in education matters.

There are many tempting offers to support quick fixes in education, often from experts or funders who talk at rather than with the people doing the work in schools, and that includes students. While applauding the Gates Foundation for admitting that $575 million was wasted, Minton claimed

> peripheral initiatives will not be sufficient to create a tipping point across the rest of the education ecosystem. To transform education we need to understand the ways the system is interconnected and develop a coherent approach to push from as many angles as possible. Beyond this, we also need to examine our basic assumptions about how teachers and students learn.[13]

Examining the nuances of leadership and management is part of unpacking the interconnected elements in schools. *To Lead or Manage: That Is a Question?* begs an examination of how these roles are the same and how they are different. A leader can facilitate meaningful change with a growth mindset, while a manager tends to focus on polishing the current practices and systems in schools.

Leaders need to provide cultures for teachers to thrive. Sheninger noted: "The right culture provides the spark teachers need to pursue and implement innovative practices actively in the classroom." It needs

> to be clear to teachers that they have the autonomy and support to be as innovative as they want. There is less of a focus on control and more on trust, which both lend themselves to the creation of a school culture molded by empowerment.[14]

The job descriptions of those in positions of responsibility in schools and school districts can play a key role in moving school improvement in a forward direction. The job posting for an administrative position can reveal the values of a system. If there are more expectations listed that focus on sustaining operational tasks, that infer a "helping" role, and use the word "maintain" or follow procedures, then such responsibilities might be considered more managerial. If the description uses words such as "building," "initiative," "collaborating," or "teaching," then such expectations might be fitting of a leader.

Table 15.1 compares school head/principal job descriptions posted for an independent school in Canada and a charter school in Florida. Expectations for such key roles in schools will often blend a mix of managerial and leadership descriptors.

The job description of a school administrator reveals whether the Board and the individual in the lead role values managing or leading. In the real world, the principal is one who needs to wear many hats, some that require the safe operating precision of management, and others that should inspire school improvement. Table 15.2 is an example of school leader job description that is heavily weighted towards action and innovation.

By examining the job descriptions of school administrators, it is possible to predict how committed a school culture and organization is dedicated to change. Gatekeepers are more comfortable with managers in administration. The antithesis of a gatekeeping manager is a school leader who models not only a growth mindset but significant action that leads to school change. As Sheninger advised:

Table 15.1. Lead or Manage Job Description Expectations in Two Schools

Independent School (Canada)	Lead	Manage	Charter School (Florida)	Lead	Manage
Maintain and build on the strong existing relationships across the school and broader community	*	*	Implementing and actively modeling, promoting, and nurturing the mission, vision and core virtues	*	
Help to renew and shape PRA's vision and mission		*	Providing reports regularly to Optima and the board of directors.		*
Support in the development and lead in the implementation of the new strategic plan	*		Maintaining a school atmosphere of academic excellence, civility, trustworthiness, respect, fairness, and equality.		*
Build on PRA's strengths, which have been integral in creating a unique and special school environment	*		Planning, implementing, supervising, and evaluating all other academic programs, i.e., extracurricular and co-curricular.		*
Embrace how foundation will continue to enhance PRA's future	*		Assuring that all academic components of the school's charter are being met.		*
Attract and retain staff	*		Setting instructional priorities and goals.		*
Ensure financial sustainability and consistency of the school		*	Ensuring alignment of curriculum with state standards.		*
Support staff engagement and professional development		*	Reviewing teacher lesson plans and instruction to ensure compliance with standards, the school's mission, and the charter contract.		*
Develop the school's enrollment strategy and marketing/communications plan	*		Planning, implementing, and evaluating the school instructional program based on the student needs, the curriculum guide, and Florida Standards.		*

Task			Task		
Pursue CAIS accreditation		*	Recruiting high quality instructional faculty for the school as needed.	*	
Develop and continue to update school policies		*	Building collaborative relationships among faculty, staff, and families of the school.	*	
Ensure effective and timely communication among all community members		*	Determining staffing needs including selection, supervision, professional development, and evaluation of school instructional personnel.		*
			Managing state assessment procedures and compliance.		*
			Ensuring the school is operating within the set instructional budget.		*
			Overseeing proper academic record keeping processes.		*
			Maintaining records such as but not limited to student test scores, attendance records, overseeing IEPs, and other reports as needed for efficient operation of the school and compliance with federal, state, and local requirements.		*
			Enforcing the policies and procedures of the organization as set by Optima and the board of directors, including the student code of conduct.		*
			Developing & implementing school rules and regulations in keeping with policies and procedures.		*
			Attending and participating in meetings of the board and its committees as requested.		*
			Maintaining knowledge of charter school laws and statutes.		*
			Ensuring the school is operating within the set instructional budget.		*

Table 15.2. School Leadership Expectations for a DC Charter School

Charter School (DC)	Lead	Manage
Models the expectations of the school norms/commitment	*	
Meets monthly with Board Chair		*
Develops school vision while sustaining school mission	*	*
Leads the coordination and implementation of the School Improvement Plan	*	
Maintains open door policy for staff, parents, and students for easy direct access to administration		*
Establishes the school calendar with input from staff and students	*	
Collaborates with and develops school leaders and the School Leadership Team	*	
Coordinates the recruitment, hiring, and retention of exceptional teachers and non-instructional staff	*	
Models lifelong learning by attending relevant seminars, conferences, and career fairs	*	
Liaises with experts at local, national, and global university institutions.	*	
Coaching, supervising, and evaluating staff through informal classroom visits	*	*
Team teaches innovative programs with teachers in classrooms.	*	
Manages, supervises, and evaluates effective personnel management and assignment of duties		*
Coaches, mentors, supports, and evaluates the VP, Academic Program	*	*
Establishes team building and facilitates rapport with peers, staff, students, parents, external stakeholders	*	
Establishes and maintains effective school/community relations through communication, outreach, and collaboration	*	*
Conducts and coordinates professional learning with teacher leaders	*	
Fosters positive school climate, and productive staff morale	*	
Nominates and recognizes committed staff for awards	*	
Supports the Parent Association and coordinates school volunteers	*	
Coordinates, communicates, and promotes effective school spirit events and assemblies	*	
Promotes effective extra-curricular activities		*
Coordinates and develops Student Council and Ambassadors	*	
Coordinates a Student Leadership Conference for student leaders	*	
Participates in student support team meetings		*
Responsible for disciplinary action and proactive reduction in disciplinary incidents	*	*
Teach Leadership class/course	*	
Collaborates with families to coordinate graduation events	*	
Leads the School Culture Team (School climate coordinator; Student Recognition and Awards Coordinator . . .)	*	
Coordinates the painting of murals to inspire students, staff, and families	*	

Move away from telling people what to do, and instead take them where they need to be. If you want change, model it. Modelling the way is one of the best things a leader can do to move others down a different path to initiate and sustain change.[15]

He added: "I made concerted efforts to roll up my sleeves, learn alongside students and staff, and show my vested interest in being part of the change process, not just an empty suit, barking out directions through impersonal means of communication.[16]

Gatekeepers can be empty suits who tend not to support efforts to increase the critical mass of teacher-leaders in schools; they are content with models that have one administrator for upwards of thirty direct reports. According to Lucy, "I want to start weekly or monthly one-on-one check ins with staff (25 people total)." The hierarchy of responsibility typically lands everything related to evaluation and feedback on the laps of the school administrators, who in the dated industrial model of schooling, simply can't keep up with all the demands of their jobs. According to Smith:

When the school leader takes on the responsibility of observing and appraising too many staff members, it is likely the evaluations will be so general in nature that they may not lead to professional growth. Often the lack of connection to specific expectations and customized professional learning, the quality of many appraisals can lack substance or any recommendations for change.[17]

Like Lucy, many school leaders recognize the inter-connectedness of feedback and professional learning, and when they can build a leadership team to provide such support, it is possible to make meaningful change happen.

A school organization chart does not have be designed in the same pattern as another school, nor should it be. A system could embrace org charts that reflect the unique missions and visions of different schools. Typically, a school has a principal who, depending on the number of students, is assigned one of more "assistant principals," who divide the tasks amongst the leadership team. There may be other roles such as department heads, special education coordinators, and athletic directors, but rarely do such medium-level leaders take part in teacher appraisals or the design and implementation of the overall school improvement plan.

The top-down model can spread out responsibilities more when a school, regardless of size, creates a larger leadership team. For instance, roles such as Vice Principal, School Culture; Vice Principal, Academics; Vice Principal, School Operations; Dean of Special Education; Dean of Professional Learning; and Dean of Fine Arts were established at a performing arts school in DC. Populated by over four hundred students and fifty teachers, the lead team reported to the principal/executive director who mentored, supported, and evaluated them in both their leadership and teaching roles.

It was feasible to expand the leadership team, when each member, including the principal, was assigned responsibilities for teaching students in their own classrooms on a part-time basis. Not only did teachers have a more dedicated mentor, students did not have to lose the opportunity to be taught by such talented teachers. In *Teacher Shortages and the Challenge of Retention: Practices that Make School Systems and Cultures More Attractive and Empowering,* Smith described this experience as follows:

> Mentors were given their own class for half a day, but were free in the other half of the school day to provide support to their mentees. One hour each week the mentor and the mentee met to co-plan a lesson, and the following day, they co-taught the lesson together in the mentee's classroom. The professional conversations when planning were grounded in the context of their co-teaching experiences in the classrooms.[18]

Inferring that such experiences can add meaning to their work, Smith noted in another book:

> Rather than relying on a few demonstrations and professional conversations, schools might consider expanding the coaching role to include regular co-planning followed by co-teaching so that supervisors and mentors can gain a deeper understanding of the classroom context, and therefore, more able to provide rich feedback for teachers, both informally, and formally.[19]

A principal and assistant principal may split a staff up to provide mentor support, but when the numbers are more than eight, the quality and quantity of support can be superficial. Given all the administrative responsibilities, the current school organization does not seem to meet the needs of students or teachers. It is much easier to fly under the radar when school leaders have too many teachers to supervise.

Gatekeepers recognize that if managers are more observers and not necessarily initiators of action, that they will not be looking for such qualities in their performance appraisals. Managers want to keep everyone happy; they do not want to rock the boat, which leaders will do when their sights are focused on school improvement for all community members. A leader will find a way to help their team embrace change, so they can grow and improve as key drivers in a school.

"Challenge your team to help them grow."

—Captain Jean-Luc Picard

NOTES

1. D. Rockwell (2022, October 12), Twitter.
2. E. C. Sheninger (2016), *Uncommon learning: Creating schools that work for kids*, p. 13.
3. R. Owen (2022, April 21), Can we make real, transformative change in education?, *Greater Good Magazine,* https://greatergood.berkeley.edu/article/item/can_we_make_real_transformative_change_in_education.
4. Owen, Can we make real, transformative change in education?
5. E. C. Lee (2019), *Stop politically driven education: Subverting the system to build a new school model*, p. 1.
6. Lee, *Stop politically driven education,* p. 5.
7. K. Easey (2022, September 12), LinkedIn.
8. Sheninger, *Uncommon learning,* p. 31.
9. Sheninger, *Uncommon learning,* p. 190.
10. B. J. Smith (2023, in press), *Teacher shortages and the challenge of retention: Practices that make school systems and cultures more attractive and empowering.*
11. Anvi (2021, May 12), How academia & its jargons gatekeep knowledge & uphold class-caste divide, Feminism in India, https://feminisminindia.com/2021/05/12/academia-jargon-gatekeep-knowledge-class-caste-divide/.
12. Anvi, How academia & its jargons gatekeep knowledge & uphold class-caste divide.
13. W. Minton (2019, October 29), What Bill Gates doesn't understand about supporting teachers, LinkedIn, https://www.linkedin.com/pulse/what-bill-gates-doesnt-understand-supporting-teachers-william-minton/.
14. Sheninger, *Uncommon learning,* p. 32.
15. Sheninger, *Uncommon learning,* p. 30.
16. Sheninger, *Uncommon learning,* p. 29.
17. Smith, *Teacher shortages and the challenge of retention.*
18. Smith, *Teacher shortages and the challenge of retention.*
19. B. J. Smith (2021), *How much does a great school cost? School economies and school values.*

Chapter 16

Leadership in Designing a New School

John Neretlis

What possesses someone to open a private school in the middle of a pandemic? In business parlance, why try to solve a problem in an industry with more barriers to entry than one could imagine, and at a time that brightly flashed failure? Well, the fact of the matter is that someone was me, and as an entrepreneur, there was a case to be made that customers needed a solution to educating their children in an industry that has barely changed in the last century.

I believe my journey to making this decision began almost fifty years ago, when I first started at JR Wilcox Public School in Toronto. I loved school and the environment there, and subsequently in middle school and high school, was one of self-determination, opportunity, and encouragement. It was a time when we were allowed and encouraged to take risks and when teachers were allowed to do what made sense to make sure we learned. This situation was echoed in the real world when I worked part-time after-school and on weekends. At no time did I ever feel like someone else was stopping me from exploring and reaching my full potential . . . there were no gatekeepers.

As I moved on with university, a military career, and many small businesses, the gatekeepers started to appear. However, with a little ingenuity and support from a variety of people throughout my life, I had the confidence to take them on to get to where I wanted to go.

Fast forward to March 2020, and what was I going to do with a small sideline business I had been running for a couple of years? *Brick Labs Inc.* was a LEGO-based entertainment/ education facility. We ran after school programs, parties, and camps. We also started venturing into schools to do some STEM based programs. We were having fun and most importantly, our customers kept returning. But when our doors were forced closed, due to the recent COVID pandemic, we had to pivot but the gatekeepers were waiting in the wings.

As we brainstormed ideas, we came face to face with the most insane rules and regulations that existed pre-pandemic and a public service system that couldn't chew gum and walk at the same time. Families (parents and children) needed help and politicians and public servants were closed to any type of sensible solutions. For example, in the early days of lockdown, childcare could only be provided to front line workers. A few of our clients who were doctors reached out to us to look after their children so they could work. They trusted us.

We quickly put into place all COVID protocols, but within two days, the government said healthcare workers had to use only government approved facilities . . . facilities that were being crammed full of kids (no social distancing) and nowhere close to where our clients lived and worked. Well we navigated those first few months and when August rolled around, our clients had a problem . . . they didn't trust the schools to keep their kids safe and wanted us to look after them. Heck, we did more than that, we started to run curriculum for our group of 12 children. We called it the *Learning Continuity Program* and it broke all the rules. Not for COVID safety, but the ones that were set up pre-pandemic for educating children and "keeping them safe."

We just did what the experts had been saying for years: small classes, experiential learning, outdoor time, a joyful environment, and individualized learning plans. The results: our students grew socially and emotionally; and they excelled academically beyond the requirements of their grade level. Additionally, our parents were happy. We had something here and it was time to take this idea to the next level: Brick Labs Academy. Enter the gatekeepers!

Gatekeeper Number One: The Ministry of Education. To obtain a Private School number in Ontario you must open your school and enroll at least five students. Then and only then can you obtain the school number and operate. In other words, make the investment first and then we'll let you know if you can run! Not exactly enticing as a business venture. The advantage we had was we already had a facility and client base to tap into.

Gatekeeper Number Two: Parents. We quickly realized even with all the data out there on the performance of students in public education, parents still believed that "the curriculum" was the standard we should be teaching to. Our future-focused STEM curriculum seemed a little out there for many. And it was definitely not for girls.

When September rolled around, we had eight full-time students from kindergarten to grade 5 and we were able to obtain our school number and operate as a private school. The year once again proved successful for our students, excelling well past anyone's expectations. In addition to the small class sizes, we attribute the success to a number of the initiatives we took.

- Initiative 1: 8-Hour Day
  First, we operate with an 8-hour school day (8.30 a.m. to 4:30 p.m.), because that's what parents need. It is not too much for students when the day is structured on our second initiative: the *Hour-In Hour-Out* (HIHO) schedule.
- Initiative 2: HIHO
  We are outside daily three times for about an hour doing free play, sports, lessons, or just going for a walk. It's amazing how ready the students are to learn again when they get back inside.
- Initiative 3: No Homework
  With the amount of time we have at school, we can ensure the children are mastering the material. Families are thrilled not to have to deal with the stress of getting homework done each night and on weekends.
- Initiative 4: Extensive Communication with Parents
  Brick Labs Academy is committed to communicating about how their child is doing. Daily at drop-off and pickup, weekly newsletters, monthly expositions of their work for parents to see, and quarterly parent/teacher/student meetings for goal setting. Students know we are all working together for their best interests.
- Initiative 5: No Standardized Testing
  Standardized testing or testing for testing's sake is something we do not do. We monitor students' work daily and have them "fail forward." We never let a mistake go by without a discussion of a lesson learned. Our students quickly understand that risk taking or trying something out is not something to be scared of.
- Initiative 6: Individualized Learning
  Finally, individualized learning strategies are worked on for each student. Yes it's a little more work for us to adapt a lesson that works for all, but it is so worth the effort when students grasp and master the material.

All of these efforts and initiatives are in a business sense, just good customer service. Sounds a bit strange when talking about education, but I think it is a huge competitive advantage for us, and one that challenges the gatekeepers' mindset about what school should be.

Being able to think about my school in this way was one of the reasons I chose to operate as a private vs. a nonprofit entity. For the last six years, I had sat on the board of a nonprofit school. While the board can assist greatly, they actually can act as another gatekeeper, ensuring that operations do not stray too far from the norms of non-public education. As an entrepreneur, I would find this additional level of oversight stifling and it would take away from the nimbleness of making necessary changes.

Gatekeeper Number Three: Students. In the early years of opening this new school, I discovered a third gatekeeper . . . the student. Not all our students have acted like gatekeepers, but those who are older and attended public school were locked in a mindset of what school should be. Teachers teach, students do work, year progresses, they get report cards, life goes on. For these older students it can take us three to four months to get them to understand that their job is to learn; that mistakes are when learning happens; and that at this school they are not being judged by teachers or students. When they stop locking out opportunities to learn, we know we have eliminated their gatekeeper within.

I can't let this last point go unsaid . . . I love coming to our building every day. Our space has been purposefully built to be joyful, with something fun and exciting to see at every turn. And our students feel the same way because they contribute to our displays and surroundings regularly. Their personalities and creativity are built right into the environment they spend forty hours per week in. It becomes a second home, and maybe they have put more in to this space than the one they go home to every night. If you love to be somewhere, it's hard not to be engaged and perform at your best.

Now into our third year (second officially), and with the pandemic behind us, we are examining how to grow our micro-school to a level that makes true business sense while not losing the sense of community, joy, and learning that is happening so freely today. We're not out to change the world or disrupt the entire education system, but a closer look at what's happening here by some gatekeepers, just may accomplish the latter.

* * *

John Neretlis, Head of School, Brick Labs Academy, Toronto, Canada

Chapter 17

Political Correctness

Barbara J. Smith

It would be an oversimplification to see the choices in education as either right or left of center. While the right voices may say that the absolute implementation of freedom of speech overrides the idea of political correctness, there are views, as spoken by more liberal progressives, which can be dismissed as not politically correct by individuals on the right side of the political spectrum. It could be argued that fixed positions on both sides of the two-dimensional continuum contribute to polarizing directions for education.

The notion of teaching basics as a foundational goal of education has been pitted at odds with the teaching of progressive education, that moves to transform education, not re-form it. Continuous improvement efforts in a transmission-oriented school tend to be fixated on management of what is known, not what students can construct or create. Standardized tests formalize the worldview that education is fixed and the memorization of content leads to a well-educated society.

The lack of a coordinated effort to define a progressive education can also make it difficult to synthesize an overwhelming body of change initiatives. Within the left transformative-focused schooling efforts, there are competing factions about "how" and "what" is considered progressive. More complicated are the educators who try to live somewhere in a balanced school world, trying to be everything for everyone, often succumbing to keeping the wheels churning on a superficial education experience.

Those who relate to the far right of politics may not understand or accept the value of critical and creative thinking. It is, however, a compelling argument that a future society will need to have the capacity to solve problems that are not laid out on pages in a textbook. Schools must provide teaching and learning spaces that prepare students for much more than performing well on multiple choice tests. Biden's quote, "Show me your budget and I'll tell you what you value," does speak about funding what you value.

Finely tuning this message to accommodate for schools, this statement might be elaborated on to emphasize the distribution of not only funding, but how time and responsibilities are distributed: "Show us the line items on a school budget, how time is organized, how teachers are respected, and how students experience an authentic education, and we'll show you what we value."

The rush to condemn "woke" by some people may have struck a nerve for many who believe that social justice should not be part of a school curriculum; it is, however, part of many real-world settings for students, so closing the gates on this authentic context runs counter to peer-reviewed research. In such learning environments, students learn to not be racist, to not use offensive language, and to not accept stereotypes that may or may not be present in their own homes.

Students are free to learn and embrace the notion that all people are created equal. While the freedom to not use words that hurt others may seem to infringe on young people's rights, so is driving on the wrong side of the road and not paying taxes. Is it a bad thing that students learn that there are laws, and school values that respect all people?

Waking up to injustice as a warranted response is not a wrong context for teaching and learning. In fact, it's probably not enough to be aware; ideally students should do something proactive to make the world a better place. It is difficult to point fingers when you are giving service to others. There is much to learn in the community if students can be freed from their industrial jail cells to be present in service learning and apprenticeship programs.

Supporters on the right tend to view school experiences such as extra-curricular activities, student leadership, character education, health education, community-based learning, and electives as promoting "soft skills," but this couldn't be further from the truth. Such courses support students in college, the world of work, and in life. Getting along and supporting others are powerful life skills that contribute to keeping and moving forward in their career and life satisfaction.

It makes sense that a liberal education defends such programs, but the limited time and status afforded to such experiences in many school systems tend to pay them more lip-service than dedicated support. Even though the research on the value of such authentic experiences is well documented, many school systems turn a blind eye to it, and permit the over-weighting of a transmission-oriented education implemented by teacher-directed methods. While there are progressive teachers in classrooms that apply solid research, it is rare for systems to do so.

Even though it seems like schools have their GPS set on progressive targets, both liberal and conservative mindsets accept standardized tests as a significant measure of quality schooling. Numerical chunks of data are valued more than qualitative accounts of transforming experiences, even though research about "quality" should use qualitative metrics.

Comparing schools that promote fixed versus growth mindsets, using quantitative tools, is like comparing apples and oranges; findings that compare uncommon denominators should not be taken seriously. Higher education has a bigger role to play in clarifying such a message, as it should in speaking up about critical race theory. Author and Director of *Creative Leadership Solutions*, Douglas B. Reeves, wrote a compelling article about censorship, which has been included in the next chapter.

The freedom to debate is a hallmark of a democratic society. To model the process of building an effective argument requires students to learn about the varied sides to a story. When books are forbidden, it limits the options for fully understanding perspectives. Teachers have the common sense to not choose pornographic material for their students to examine, as such texts or images can be demeaning and offensive.

When politicians censor books, they take a position to not only control curriculum, but distrust the professional capacity of teachers. Diane Ravitch noted in her blog: "The overwhelming number of banned books deal with race and gender. The censors apparently think that no one will learn about race or gender if no books are available."[1] The website pen.org reveals a concern about the forces that are committed to the gatekeeping of books from being used by teachers and students:

> the large majority of book bans underway today are not spontaneous, organic expressions of citizen concern. Rather, they reflect the work of a growing number of advocacy organizations that have made demanding censorship of certain books and ideas in schools part of their mission.[2]

The extent of book banning in the United States varies from state to state. Fifteen states do not ban any books, whereas Texas has listed over 750 books. The nature of the books banned in the United States include "674 titles (41 percent) explicitly address LGBTQ+" and "659 titles (40 percent) contain protagonists or prominent secondary characters of color."[3] For those who worship data, what discussions should happen as a result of these statistics? Any free country identifying as a democracy might think twice about such *Fahrenheit 451*–like warnings, that should be fiction.

English teacher Sheryl Lain shared how her school board called her "on the carpet" for teaching John Steinbeck's *The Grapes of Wrath*[4] (1939) to her senior students. She noted: "This experience taught me a lesson: teaching language arts and literacy means teetering on the edge of the box."[5] Ideas, hidden from view, limit the opportunities for students and teachers to think about alternative perspectives or understand the historical forces at play. In The Thinking School, Dr. Kulvarn Atwal tweeted a warning about schools sticking to a script: "On a podcast in the US, I was told that some teachers are given scripts to teach and monitored to ensure they stick to that script.. . . . "[6] After forty years of teaching, Lain shared her worries:

> I see a trend to narrow the English language arts curriculum by requiring teachers to follow scripted lessons, testing students using purchased standardized tests, and, de-valuing poetic and expressive writing, all of which strangles teacher autonomy and dulls the vitality of student writing. I offer this antidote to teachers: Go off script. Step out of the box.[7]

Concerned about approaches that expect teachers to mimic scripts, Sidebottom tweets concern about ethical issues: "Discussing the de-professionalisation of teachers via scripted lessons and establishment of fixed routines today. It's a global issue which increases the likelihood of automation, alongside privatisation/profiteering by large educational conglomerates."[8] The idea that teachers should memorize scripts to improve their practice is the antithesis of quality professional learning, and more conducive to "training" a zoo performer. As Lee noted:

> A new view of teacher accountability is essential to improving the quality of the system of education. The reality is that current accountability measures are based on the unethical "teach to the test" mentality that ultimately silences innovators while forcing them to follow scripted lessons.[9]

To write without the fear of coloring outside the lines of a district, provincial, or state department of education, is much easier when retired from such affiliations. Writers often think twice about how blunt to be for fear of being criticized or losing their job if superiors interpret the text as challenging their position. The idea that all must "row in the same direction" is a real concern when writers are part of a larger organization. A writer must wonder, for instance, how a publisher might respond to challenges of an over-reliance on textbooks in schools.

Fear of how others might interpret one's words and actions is a gatekeeper of the political correctness kind. In response to criticism, there is also a handy deck of cards frequently used by gatekeepers to keep innovative ideas from seeping in. Voices fearful of change in school communities will often hold up the safety card, the legal card, the technology card, and the equity card to grind change to a halt. An innovator will be wise to consider the collateral damage of change to ensure that it can be implemented in a productive and meaningful way, with few, if any casualties.

How often have questions been raised about risk management when innovative ideas for schools are presented for consideration? The ramifications of any change to the physical plant, the staffing roles, or the student schedules—all can bring about scenarios of risk. Anticipating and limiting risks in advance of innovative proposals is a logical step for change agents. Often the fear that the change cannot be safely implemented will shut down an idea. It may be a rational fear, or it may be irrational; the perception of stakeholders matters, whether justified or not. Experts may help alleviate anxiety, but there is no guarantee.

Any administrator who has tried to make a family or employee handbook a tool for communicating innovation has found that the legal matter embedded within such texts can contribute to fixed conditions for operating, and in doing so, limit or eliminate the opportunity for innovation. Finding a way for the legal system to adapt and support more flexible school operations could help limit the use of the legal card as a reason for why something new cannot be done.

The technology card has often been used to explain why many new initiatives cannot happen in schools. Even though the computer was supposed to make things easier, the limits of software programming make it a challenge to revise schedules, report cards, and a host of automated activities including the length of parent-teacher conferences. The echo, "We can't change because the technology won't support it" may sound off, but there is always new technology that can be designed, to support an innovative school, rather than confine it.

The equity card is delicate, because many decisions in schools can be interpreted as inequitable. When schools address innovation from a fairness perspective, it is possible to view equity in a timely way. In one school board in the mid-eighties, the middle schools were all scheduled to have single gymnasiums replaced with double gyms. The budget enabled the building of 115 gyms over a five-year period. The schools were not renovated at the same time. Not equitable, but fair. An equitable viewpoint would have all 115 schools spend the same budget allocation on smaller physical education equipment, never benefitting from a central coordinated effort that over time gave all middle school students in the board larger gymnasiums.

Do all students need to have chess lessons or have robotics in a K-8 school each year? No, but often programs are not permitted unless every student can take part. The "equity" card is ironically used to limit access to field trips or for supporting professional learning opportunities for teachers. When the costs are put back on the students or teachers, of course, it creates conditions where some can afford an experience and others cannot.

If visiting the beaches of Normandy is what is required to understand World War II, then budgets need to provide funds to make it happen for all students to engage in experiential learning. Re-purposing budgets for what schools value is at the heart of minimizing the impact of the equity card as a gatekeeper.

Those who rock the boat or recommend ideas out of the box are often perceived as not supporting the direction of the school, and often can be shunned by those in positions of power in an educational organization. The politics can keep all stakeholders busy attending to collateral activities, which can often strengthen the gate wall, avoiding change, and the cost of such non-action and no risk is education for all. Educators need to serve student learning, not be the servants for tool implementation.

> "Computers make excellent and efficient servants, but I have no wish to serve under them."
>
> —Spock

NOTES

1. D. Ravitch (2022, October 12), PEN America: The growing movement to ban books, https://dianeravitch.net/2022/10/12/pen-america-the-growing-movement-to-ban-books/.

2. J. Friedman (2022), Banned in the USA: The growing movement to censor books in schools, PEN America 100, https://pen.org/report/banned-usa-growing-movement-to-censor-books-in-schools/.

3. Friedman, Banned in the USA.

4. J. Steinbeck (1939), *The grapes of wrath*.

5. S. Lain (2017), Poetry is not out of the box, *New England Reading Association Journal*, 52 (1), 20–25, p. 20, https://www.proquest.com/docview/2405313561.

6. K. Atwal (2022, October 12), The Thinking School, Twitter.

7. Lain, Poetry is not out of the box, p. 24.

8. Sidebottom, (2022, October 11), Twitter.

9. E. C. Lee (2019), *Stop politically driven education: Subverting the system to build a new school model*.

Chapter 18

We Censor Ourselves

Douglas Reeves

When I was a teacher in China, my intern ultimately became the anchor of the evening news on China Central Television (CCTV). When she appeared at an educational forum in Cambridge, this brilliant and self-assured journalist startled the audience by saying, "We have no censorship in China." When she was challenged at this evidently absurd statement, she replied, "We do not need censorship in China. We censor ourselves." So it is in American education today.

This is not about critical race theory, a subject that is not in the curriculum of any of the fifty states. This is about benign subjects that, until recently, parents and educational leaders expected teachers to understand and teach as they had for decades. The pursuit of equity, for example, is not a political agenda, but merely an evidence-based approach to acknowledging that different students have different needs and that there are documented techniques to improve the literacy and math skills of all students. This is not about indoctrinating students that America is a fundamentally racist country, but rather about acknowledging that our founding documents, including the Constitution, which is rightly revered as the longest serving democratic governing system in history, included the three-fifths compromise. This is not about indicting Washington and Jefferson by contemporary standards, but about acknowledging the reality that both of these heroes of the Revolution owned human beings.

Yet in the contemporary hagiography of American history, these subjects are off-limits in many parts of the country. While some school officials have implemented official policies of censorship of controversial topics, the more common practice is redolent of journalists in Communist China, where censorship is unnecessary because teachers and school administrators censor themselves.

I know of no better way to ensure the absence of critical thinking of today's students and their inevitable future rebellion than to have a generation of young people who will soon realize that they were shielded from essential truths about our history. It is possible to love our country, serve in the military, and devote oneself to education, as I have, and nevertheless acknowledge our imperfections. If we believe that the purpose of education is to avoid encountering contrary views and then critically examining them, we rob our students of one of their essential roles as citizens.

The cost of self-censorship by teachers and school leaders goes beyond the stifling of intellectual arguments that are the lifeblood of democracy. These costs are revealed in the teacher attrition data in which 53 percent of teachers report that they would leave the profession if they could. The turnover rate of teachers and administrators is especially severe in high-poverty schools, leaving students and the remaining faculty with a sense of cynicism and fear.

The cost of teacher turnover is already being felt in poor urban and rural areas where the teacher shortage leaves students taught by eighteen-year-old substitute teachers with a driver's license and unburdened by any knowledge of the subject they are teaching. The inevitable result is students who are unprepared for high school, leading to a pending drop-out time bomb of students who cannot graduate. This is not a 2022 problem, but a 2062 problem, as those dropouts will face decades of poverty, unemployment, medical care costs, and involvement in the criminal justice system. These are costs that all of us—including the censors—will pay.

The Communist Chinese press and those who object to discussions of unpleasant parts of American history might mutually resent the comparison. But their methods of intimidation leading to self-censorship are the same. It is not too late to back off from the brink, teach the facts, and let our students learn.

* * *

*Douglas Reeves is a writer, researcher, and founder of Creative Leadership Solutions (*https://www.creativeleadership.net/about-us*) in Boston.*

Chapter 19

Higher Education

Barbara J. Smith

Gatekeeping can be an art form in higher education. It can happen within research protocols, admission departments, hiring and tenure practices, and expert endorsements. Educators who obtain graduate level degrees, conduct research, and author works that are grounded in respected peer review educational journals and books, are considered key educational leaders who develop new theories and directions in education.

The responsibility for generating new knowledge into improved ways of teaching and learning is a tall order. The research that informs national, provincial, state, or local district level curriculum should include how the implementation of innovative practices, can be shaped by all stakeholders, and thus transform, not only the school culture, but the curriculum itself.

Educational research can sometimes be complicit in supporting the political wave of education. In the past few decades, this includes the overreliance on high stakes testing as a measure of learning and the quality of a school. Even when researchers are aware of the limitations of standards and testing, they tend not to challenge the status quo, which is what experts need to do. Many academics who populate positions in higher education could be viewed as bystanders, lacking courage to denounce gatekeeping practices in education.

Just as K-12 schools can lead or follow, so too can institutions of higher learning do the same. Universities and colleges can embrace changes in their admissions, course offerings, staffing, grading, and teacher-preparation programs. Given the value afforded to higher education, it would be expected that such learning spaces be incubators of innovation and free thought. Some higher education institutions more than others promote and emit critical and creative thinking. Those that do have found a way to open the gates of sameness to make room for innovative practices.

To be admitted to an institution of higher education requires a number of steps depending on the college. The *U.S. News* ranks each university based mainly on their average SAT scores. Even though some admission departments have made it optional to submit these standardized tests scores, there compilation and averages of these results enters into school rankings.

As recommended in the first chapter, "Rapid Tests," high school students should be encouraged to create and submit portfolios for college admission consideration. Rather than complete the lengthy Common Application[1] in the United States, portfolios could better feature what students do for others, how they take part in extracurricular activities, and what makes them unique. Portfolios should also house reference letters for students from teachers and other trusted adults in their lives. Populating a fixed software program with data limits the opportunity for decision-makers to view how potential candidates can demonstrate initiative and creativity.

At the graduate level, admission teams are looking for students who have the capacity to analyze research, and use it to create compelling arguments. At one time most graduate students in education were required to conduct research and complete a thesis. Some supervisors who took on apprentice roles to support graduate researchers would help by providing opportunities for the newcomers to co-publish articles and books with them. These higher education professionals did more than focus on their work. They had the insight to see that newcomers had foresight, experience, and potential to contribute to academia.

On the other hand, the tangled world of higher education has cemented a variety of practices that support gatekeeping. The thesis has to be formatted a certain way, with formal glue binding. At one time discs and digital artifacts could not be included in the document submission. A music educator, for instance, who wanted to share evidence of a student's composition transformations as performed on a piano, was not able to submit this more integrated and authentic evidence. Even after an appeal process, the gates remained closed. There was only one way the thesis could be presented.

The journey from newcomer to expert in academia is often viewed as an individual journey beginning with the thesis, leading to a compilation of individually penned articles. What seems at odds with the theory of learning that promotes social interaction, is the steadfast support of individual products in higher education. As Reeves noted: "Universities require that doctoral candidates studying collaborative learning write their dissertations entirely alone."[2]

The process surrounding the selection of tenure-track faculty and the notion of tenure itself is often challenged, but few in positions of responsibility stick their head out to explore alternatives. Different schools customize their matrixes for various levels of ranks within a university: full professor, assistant professor, associate professor, and instructors, usually seconded from a local school board, but the clear line of hierarchy is nevertheless an accepted condition of employment.

Educators can also take part in graduate programs that can include specialist and principal qualifications. Some may pursue an Education Doctorate (ED), which does not always meet the requirements of working in higher education. Other educators enroll in PhD (Doctor of Philosophy) programs with a focus in one or more areas of study. What happens in schools can be influenced by the research that comes from distinct silos in education such as leadership and higher education, curriculum, teaching and learning, cognitive science, counselling, and other focus areas formulated by schools of education.

Often distinct peer-reviewed journals support one education silo or another, using specific manuscript rules for how content is to be shared. Authors of articles are often invited to sit on editorial review boards, which usually involves taking turns at reviewing articles submitted for publication. Some journals are like fortresses with little room for new players, unless anointed by a successful member. The use of third person, as an industry standard, further distances the writer from their own experiences.

The idea of "blind review" built into the journal publishing process makes it all seem fair to those on the inside, but such reviews can weed out innovative ideas that seem foreign to those residing outside the trenches. Many of the people reviewing exist outside the context of education, yet they hold significant positions that grant or deny the entry of new possibilities into the world of educational research.

Many experts often write about cases of transformation in other writing spaces such as books and manuals, but the gatekeepers in review roles have been the source of thwarting new ideas for many decades. What happens to the hybrids with solid backgrounds in educational research who apply their understandings in real schools? Are they invited to the party? Are they selected as reviewers for these journals? Are they hired as instructors or adjunct professors in schools of education?

Some professionals begin their own journals to navigate around the gates of rejection, and while more options give more educators more opportunities to publish, it still does not address the sameness of a system committed to competition for space. There are articles in professional journals where many practitioners share case stories and experience. What if those in positions of responsibility in higher education institutions read and referenced these firsthand accounts?

The gap between theory and practice is not simply a matter of finding a way for practitioners to talk about the messages from academia; rather, it might have more to do with the lack of trust in researchers who live outside the teaching world, living from article to article in a publish or perish world of higher education. It is surprising that with all that is written about the damaging impact of ranking, that a culture in higher education would be so compliant in accepting the reality of writing for journals that pride themselves on high rejection rates.

Many reviewers have mastered the art of rejection. Few address the material with any sense of compassion. Some comments can be ruthless like an episode of *Game of Thrones*, as if the pen is a power tool made for decimating the soul of those silly enough to think they are capable of being amongst the greats. Gatekeeping lives in the hallowed halls of many who control the peer-review processes in educational journals. After all, to be considered for tenure-track positions, research must have a solid publishing record in peer-reviewed journals.

It comes easy for some reviewers to find fault in any piece of writing. It could be argued that more intellect is required to find the strength in a piece of work. Some reviewers offer mid-range responses that suggest that authors can make changes and re-submit. Unlike the relationship between a thesis supervisor and a young researcher, often the feedback is so general it can be impossible for the recipient to read the reviewer's mind. How many writers actually re-submit? How many don't? Would such data be taken into account when selecting reviewers? Accountability needs not be designed in a vertical top-down direction.

The adage—"that's just the way it is"—can be challenged and should be challenged by the people on the insides of these institutions. Design better ways to select the teachers of teachers. According to Lopez: "Tenure track at university is one of the oldest systems that marginalizes those who teach and are called 'practitioners.' This system positions those who teach at university and not on 'tenure track' as less than."[3]

What happens when newcomers approach experts to endorse their ideas? Some members of academia who make time to co-write with their students are probably more apt to write a book endorsement for others, even if they have not taught them or had direct contact with them. These remarkable professionals make time to read ideas outside of their own vision.

Many other experts might refer the request to a "middle career researcher," someone else, and many of these gatekeepers simply ignore requests for feedback or support. Those experts who respond to new and unfamiliar authors from all over the world understand their role is bigger, one that builds a community of passionate educators, writers, and researchers.

Having researchers as instructors, especially with minimal school and school leadership experience is not the answer. Each stakeholder, even the elite in teacher education, can do better. It's time to challenge such systems. Who said paired research doesn't count? Who said a researcher can't be a teacher? Who said a teacher can't be a researcher?

Education job descriptions posted for positions in higher education often share a similar need. Reading through the requirements shines a light on what many schools of education value. For instance, at one reputable institution in Toronto, applicants are informed that they should have "a clearly articulated program of research," and that:

> Candidates must provide evidence of research excellence or promise of research excellence of a recognized international caliber as demonstrated in: the research statement; a record of publications (or forthcoming publications) with significant journals in the field; and/or other scholarly productions; presentations at major conferences; awards and accolades; and strong recommendations from referees of high standing.[4]

Even though the mission of this Faculty of Education is to reinvent education "for a diverse and complex world," the path of research and scholarship might be viewed as limiting what are offered as "innovative programs." Such values, often in conflict with one another, are perhaps superseded by the underlying need for sustainability, in other words, funding.

Some schools also require that candidates submit a funding record. The provision of grants to universities makes it important to invest in professors who can bring more funds to the programs. The acquisition of research grants, like the selection of articles for peer-reviewed journals can also be highly stacked against those who do the educating inside schools. Teachers can be within the context of what is being studied for a grant, but their role as a researcher is rarely supported. How often do universities accept action or participatory research as rigor?

Students in graduate education programs can be in awe of the publication records of their professors. There are some advisors who support their students and co-publish with them, and there are others who do not. Are such professors rewarded for taking on such mentoring roles? How much time have professors spent in classrooms and do they return to classrooms to make sure their ideas link to the context of teaching and learning?

Some graduate students provide an opening for academics into the real world of classrooms. The permission to work with student and teacher subjects in schools and districts is not an easy gate for university researchers to open. As much as there is bureaucracy in higher education, it can be just as frustrating for researchers, whether teacher-researchers or not, to gain access to classrooms for educational research.

There is much talk about the learning gap between students in K-12 education, but not so much concern is raised about the distance between educational researchers and classroom teachers and students. As Dr. Watson suggests: "Most higher ed faculty were never K to 12 teachers—and it shows."[5]

Given the extent of red tape that surrounds the task of conducting research with students as subjects, often educational research is based on teachers' perceptions. Teachers who take graduate courses can often agree to be participants in studies without having to gain permission from board or district level overseers of educational research.

Having safeguards in place at the board level provides officials with the opportunity to make sure research conducted in their schools will not cause harm to the subjects. While checks and balances do need to be in place, the level of bureaucracy to gain permission to research inside schools does make it more difficult for researchers. The gap in data gathered directly from students is considerable; an examination of protocols with recommendations for revising protocols could help to increase studies that access more student voices.

The Talk Project[6] supported teachers in the Peel Board of Education to write and publish hundreds of action researcher stories. The interactions of professors, namely David Booth, from OISE at the University of Toronto with teachers were collegial; there was a tone that was less worshipping and more co-constructing, a marked difference from a lecture and absorption of the professor's content in a graduate class. Teachers were empowered, but were their stories respected and valued by academia?

Teachers in many cases told their narrative accounts of the teaching and learning in the contexts of their classrooms, not apologizing for admitting their interdependent role. Teachers did receive an additional qualification course. While such experiences did not lead most practitioners into the world of academia, they became much more empowered professionals and given the wealth of their contextual experiences had much to contribute to their local teaching and learning conditions.

The notion that a greater percentage of rejected candidates selected for graduate schools can contribute to the strength of a school should also be challenged and earmarked as conventional gatekeeping practice, as is the "publish or perish" requirement for university employment. If experiential learning is valued for students in many school systems, then it should be respected as a viable path to higher education.

What kind of rules would higher education change? How can schools of education be more innovative? What kinds of changes could be made to enhance the expert culture informing peer-reviewed journals? Would such changes increase their readership to include more practitioners? Is it possible that perspectives outside of academia might contribute to enhancing higher education? The lowering of the shields and the opening of the gates could influence the culture of higher education, faculties of education, government departments of education, research publications, and education as a whole.

"Things are only impossible until they're not."

—Captain Jean-Luc Picard

NOTES

1. Common Application, https://www.commonapp.org.
2. D. B. Reeves (2021, February 1), Five professional learning transformations for a post-COVID world, *ASCD* 78(5), https://www.ascd.org/el/articles/five-professional-learning-transformations-for-a-post-covid-world.
3. A. Lopez (2022, September 13), Twitter.
4. York University, Assistant Professor, Literacy in Early Childhood Education, Faculty of Education, York University, https://www.yorku.ca/edu/about/current-opportunities-literacy-in-early-childhood-education/.
5. Dr. Watson [@terrinwatson] (2022, October 17), Twitter.
6. Talk Project, https://www.goodreads.com/book/show/12949036-classroom-talk.

Chapter 20

Post-Secondary Education
The Presence of *Invisible Steps and Stairs*

Beverley Freedman

We think about post-secondary or higher education as an opportunity to learn, explore, and grow. Education can determine both an individual's and a nation's continued success. In their analysis, Statistics Canada found that holding post-secondary credentials improves the likelihood of sustained employment and positive outcomes.

Being involved in higher education as a student or faculty enables exposure to new ideas, engaging with diverse and interesting learners. Higher education can provide a place and space to explore, challenge, and grow. I grew up expecting to attend the University of Toronto, an institution of higher education. In fact, the World Bank identified Canada as the most educated nation globally with the greatest percentage of adults with post-secondary certification.[1]

Then, I never really considered barriers and challenges for students less served by post-secondary institutions. Experience, working with, and listening to underserved communities now has taught me to be cognizant of equity and privilege in different ways. "To be admitted to an institution of higher education requires a number of steps depending on the college," but what if the steps of the staircase are invisible to the applicant (Chapter 10)?

There is a staircase you need to climb in order to walk through that higher education door but for some the staircase is invisible. Many of the solutions require institutional and organizational fixes. I have worked for a variety of different universities as a sessional instructor. Assuming high school graduation and an interest in obtaining post-secondary certification, the application process to post-secondary institutions remains a barrier.

To begin, the process is online and requires a credit card. Working with adults completing their high school diplomas, I heard firsthand how many students do not have access to reliable internet, digital tools, and a credit card. Some high schools will have a process for students to use the school or staff credit cards (with reimbursement) and access to computers with councilors to assist. But for many students the stairs are invisible and not able to be negotiated so the portals/doors are closed.

For those who are immigrants and refugees they may not have access to their records in their home countries. Their lack of English fluency may be a restriction since applications and the online sites require a high degree of fluency and comprehension. Some post-secondary institutions have access to translation but it isn't ubiquitous and if you don't understand what is being asked, the stairs going up are invisible. If you don't have access to translators in your primary language or translated materials, how do you know where the stairs are? How can you climb to your desired goal?

International students face issues of racism and discrimination especially from racialized minorities. They may have restrictions on work and co-op experiences and struggle to meet increasing financial demands.

Here are some examples of additional challenges I know applicants have faced:

- Understanding exactly which documents are required by the applicant but also by the institution in a foreign country forwarding the credentialing.
- An applicant who had worked in Saudi but was not a citizen and there was no response in terms of substantiated credentials to enter college for anyone other than a Saudi citizen.
- The first in the family to consider higher education and there are no role models to help navigate the system. She didn't even think higher education was a possibility until her teachers urged her to apply. Her family wasn't supportive.
- For refugees, documentation left behind or documents that were destroyed when schools/offices were bombed and burned. There is no ability to verify claims of previous educational experiences. That was what a colleague of mine experienced when her family fled Afghanistan.
- Foreign institutions that do not feel the urgency to respond to the North American higher education institutions for validation and/or clarification, in what we in the west see as "timely." A friend found it took three years for her institution to respond to an education program in Canada.

- Difficulty in Canadian post-secondary institutions assessing, evaluating, and judging equivalency from other countries and programs.

My consulting work with remote and rural communities has shown me that reliable access to internet is sketchy, which is a limiting factor in applying for and accessing materials and courses online. The cost of higher education may be prohibitive for families at or below the poverty level. They may not understand how to access grants/loans that exist to ease their way up those stairs. They don't know where to begin. When you come from a community of a few hundred or even a thousand moving to a large urban center may be scary and lonely.

For many families, the cost is prohibitive. They and their families may not be able to afford rent, books, and supplies and may be food vulnerable. The families/individuals may face other priorities. They may not be aware of subsidies and grants that exist to support applicants like them. They may be reluctant to take out loans. They may see the staircase but the steps are too high to climb.

For some lower socioeconomic and remote schools, academic language may not be as well embedded in their schoolwork, so they are disadvantaged in not only the application process but then the expectations on research and ongoing school work. They may not have had access to modernized labs or current technology to work with and so may be disadvantaged in those areas and so the staircase is not easy to identify or steps to climb.

Additionally, they may be the first in their family/community to apply. I have several friends and colleagues where this was true. In my experience, this was especially relevant for women, who were not seen as equal to their male siblings and not given the same encouragement or support. There may be a lack of mentorship of individuals who have successfully navigated those invisible stairs and succeeded, so learners in these communities may not see themselves as a potential higher education candidate.

For First Nation and other Indigenous communities the impact of the residential school system and systemic racism have led to multigenerational trauma. Dr. Maggie Jones measured the economic intergenerational damage resulting from the imposition of the residential school system. Her research concluded that those who attended residential schools had a lower high school graduation rate, which then negatively impacted their lifetime economic earning potential. She links this persistent multigenerational trauma arising from the residential school system to two factors:

- A lack of strong parental models resulting from forcible separation,
- A "sense of distrust in mainstream educational institutions that has persisted across generations"[2]

Microaggressions and systemic racism exist. Institutions of higher education must be proactive and aware of what is happening in their own institution by other students and faculty. I have experienced comments and have heard from my students about demeaning comments that profs made about "you people" or "those people." This includes disparaging comments diminishing their heritage and identity. White privilege does exist as does discrimination against gender identity.

Another group that finds access to those invisible stairs challenging are those with identified and/or non-identified learning issues. For accommodations to be recognized in higher education, many institutions require an Individual Education Plan (IEP). Some families are resistant to identification and others don't have an IEP that is current. If the diversity is physical, then not all buildings are accessible. Students may require access to specialized technology, interpreters, and interveners. Institutions have departments focused on a range of supportive student services; however you need to be both proactive and aware of the services to access them. Professors may lack the skills to provide accommodations and adaptive strategies necessary to guarantee success.

There are ways to illuminate the staircase and ease the steps up to enter that door of higher education. Confront systemic barriers and racism with clear policies, and transparent consequences. Acknowledge the issues are real. Provide outreach to underserved high schools to increase awareness for students about possibilities offered by institutions of higher education. Form alliances with underserved communities and increase communication and information in many languages, including ADL. Build strategic partnerships with local agencies and organizations that serve families. Provide peer mentors and community supports in the receiving institutions to help ensure students will apply and stay and not drop out. Support affinity groups on campus. By offering onsite and virtual transitioning programs, including summer programs, students can be assisted in scaffolding those higher education steps. Make role models available—both in person and virtually so students can see the possibilities.

Increase the availability for financial subsidies, affordable housing, and childcare and make sure applicants from underserved communities are aware of existing and available supports, including student services and programs with elders that exist. Increase paid co-op opportunities for students from financially challenged communities.

By providing targeted resources for high schools including for academic writing, labs, and research the staircase is better illuminated and the students have the skills and knowledge to climb those steps. Additionally, provide targeted and responsive training for professors so they are more accommodating and adaptive to students who do not see themselves in the curriculum, resources, or programs. They need to be more aware of the systemic barriers that exist and the struggles required to climb those stairs.

What I haven't discussed are neither the invisible stairs to continuing and being successful in higher education, nor the invisible staircases to promotion. A discussion for another time. I love to learn, and I have been privileged to attend post-secondary as a student and as an instructor. I want the staircase illuminated and steps accessible to all.

* * *

Beverley Freedman, EdD, Educational Service Consulting https:// beverleyfreedman.com, former Superintendent.

NOTES

1. Jane Katkova & Associates, Now it is official. Canada is the most educated developed country in world!, https://canadianimmigrationexperts.ca/canada-is-the-most-educated-developed-country-in-world/; Canadian Bureau of International Education (2022), The student voice: National results of the 2021 CBIE international student survey, https://km4s.ca/wp-content/uploads/CBIE_2021_International_Student_Survey_National_Report.pdf.

2. M. Barber & M. E. C. Jones (2021), Inequalities in test scores between Indigenous and Non-Indigenous youth in Canada, *Economics of Education Review*, 83, p. 25.

Chapter 21

Five Days in October

Barbara J. Smith

The declining teacher morale in many schools is reminiscent of the devastating healthcare conditions at Memorial Hospital in New Orleans after the levees collapsed from the force of Hurricane Katrina in 2005. The television series *Five Days at Memorial* highlighted how rising water levels rendered a hospital helpless. While the carnage is not so immediate in schools, *Five Days in October* examines a slice of the debilitating impact of impossible teacher loads caused by the volume of curriculum, standards, and tests that continue to smother teaching and learning.

Those concerned about providing quality education need to be aware that the system is drowning in a sea of dysfunction. Fullan and Rizzotto describe the crumbling conditions for teachers today:

> Relentless, unbearable, ever-worsening pressures make it impossible, some say, for even the most dedicated teachers to remain. What if we were to say that the structural cracks had been there for some time. Like a Florida condominium or London's Grenfell Tower collapse was inevitable—just a matter of time and additional stress that became the last straw.[1]

In the 2022–23 school year, many schools boomeranged back to the grind of "normalcy" following the interruptions of the COVID pandemic. This health crisis provided an urgent rationale for keeping the gates closed to new ideas, especially initiatives that could not fit technology "delivery" modes. While Zoom provided a space for seeing faces come together and Google Docs were populated with student assignment folders, there did not seem to be an out-pouring of more schools embracing engaging learning activities such as project-based learning.

It was enough for teachers to manage new ways of communicating via a digital medium, but it would be an assumption that the use of technology was enough to change student engagement. The curriculum cup remained overfilled before, during, and after the pandemic. Students, for some time, have experienced little joy in teacher-directed, one-way communicated lectures, yet with so much content, many teachers feel they have little choice.

After the first month of a new school year, the honeymoon can wear thin for many teachers who need more energy to sustain their enthusiasm and fuel their creativity. To gain a glimpse of how teachers describe their depleted energy stores and unrealistic expectations, five days of Twitter responses about schooling were examined between October 12 and October 16.

October 12, 2022, was selected as the start day for this humble review, as this was a day when teachers in Australia wore red in solidarity of challenging their education system. Teachers were encouraged "to wear red to school and take part in a social media campaign aimed at expressing anger over the Perrottet Government's failure to address unsustainable workloads and uncompetitive salaries."[2] Whether educators wore red or left the profession, it is clear that polishing the doorknobs on the Titanic won't cut it when it comes to avoiding a decaying system.

October 12, 2022

- "If we want teachers to STAY in the classroom, we're going to have to let them teach their passions to their students. I mean . . . we're gonna have to put a pause on the boxed curriculums your districts are paying millions for and let teachers just share their passions with kids. The pedestal of the classroom becomes frightening, feedback becomes attacks, and all the systemic parts of this work that are difficult (lack of time, differentiating, shifting mandates) become overwhelming. It's a different world."—Marcus Luther[3]
- "School doesn't start for another 40 minutes and I'm already sitting here with tears in my eyes over another boxed curriculum that I'm supposed to add in."—Lauren Deal[4]
- "OMG I am 3 weeks into this boxed curriculum and it makes me want to weep. How can I possibly expect kids to be invested in something I have zero investment in? My biggest loves in teaching are creative lesson planning and kids' humor. I've lost both."—Wendy Gassaway[5]
- "Were you able to prepare all of that original curriculum - AND complete your grading and other lesson planning and caregiver contacts, etc. - during your contracted planning time? Overwork is a HUGE problem."—Dana Cole[6]

- "It's also very frustrating because there are tons of respected PD authors with lots of research backup and experience writing great books on their area of expertise, but we can't use their work because it doesn't come in a box that claims to do everything."—Altaira Morbius[7]
- "I had to read a short story last night in order to help one of my ELL students in English 11. I . . . I couldn't even force myself to read the thing. Skimmed all of it. New boxed curriculum and it's so boring."—Cheri Mann[8]
- "OMG! I have a box for the curriculum in the form of a pacing guide. Like how can an entire district be on the exact page, doing the exact exercises daily? But we're supposed to differentiate for the kids' needs? And we're not allowed to fall behind for even a hurricane!"—Ms. Carasco[9]
- "Imagine if we took all that curriculum money and redirected it towards staff- for salary, for PD funding, for materials, to send staff to conferences/classes, to update tech, etc. everything needed so teachers can teach what they love and share that excitement with kids."—Kit[10]
- "Passion breeds passion!! Let's go!! Curriculum freight train needs to come to an end!!"—William Richards[11]

October 13, 2022

- "There is a teacher shortage on its way/ It might already be here . . . This is time when staff wellbeing should be at the top of the list/ We need to keep great colleagues in our profession. We need to support our community."—Jude[12]
- "I talked with a teacher while blockwalking tonight. She confirmed that we don't have a teacher shortage; it's an exodus. We already have so many good teachers here in Texas & we need to make sure we have a suitable work environment in order to retain them."—Josh Tutt[13]
- "I'm an underpaid teacher picking up the slack during a teacher shortage. The STAAR test dictates my whole curriculum. My property taxes are ridiculous. I had to evacuate during the winter freeze with my pets and drive on dangerously icy roads to get to warmth/running water."—Sarah Lynn[14]
- "We entered the profession with aspirations of teaching for 30–40 years. Now we all have a 3–4 year exit plan"—Guy McDermott[15]

October 14, 2022

- "Pay teachers more & address the unsustainable workload. No teachers no future! . . . "—Katie Sullivan[16]

- "There's nothing you can tell me that will justify a school district paying millions and millions of dollars for curriculum."—Patrick[17]
- "Many young South African teachers are considering changing jobs. Some are looking for other options within education, some are looking at augmenting teaching incomes with other work while others plan to leave the profession entirely. This is disturbing."—Daily Maverick[18]
- "Between January 2020, and February, 2022, upward of six hundred thousand teachers have left the profession . . . more than half of teachers say they will leave teaching earlier than they originally anticipated."—The Marigold Project[19]

October 15, 2022

- "Data should be a tool for growth not a weapon for shame."—Susan Storey[20]
- "There are too many leaders in education who are too distanced from what it really means to teach well . . . too many curriculum developers who have no idea what really happens in a classroom, the need for context and meaning w/regard to curriculum planning/use."—Maureen Devlin[21]
- "Repeat after me. Teacher recruitment initiatives - a band-aid on teacher shortage. We don't need more teachers. We need a more sustainably designed job."—Lennon Audrain[22]
- "We can't have a situation where teachers are leaving our schools because they don't know whether they will have a job next term or next year. Teaching should be a job you want to stay in for your entire career."—Alice Leung[23]

October 16, 2022

- "Teachers drowning in 'near-impossible' amount of lesson planning."—Angelo Gavrielatos[24]
- "I hate a scripted curriculum . . . I am not a fricking robot . . . but perhaps that's the long term goal? Replace us all with a teacher in a box?"—@north1963[25]
- "Lol last year I did a book study of Efren Divided which my students LOVED and very much related to AND I bought the books but this year was told there will be NO MORE OF THAT stick w the curriculum"—Morgan Sanchez[26]
- "I have enough years in that I feel secure enough in my position to do what I think is best. Otherwise, I know I would feel as you do. I'm so sorry. America needs to trust teachers again."—Karen Arnold[27]

On the next day, October 17, Mrs. Hernandez tweeted: "Don't mind me just casually spiraling as I question my decision to stay in education because following our new mandated curriculum with fidelity sucks the joy away from teaching,"[28] which received 1,640 "likes" the same day. The tweets are not simply part of a string that will go away. They are a symptom of widespread illness in the education system.

The twenty-five comments included from browsing Twitter over five days reveal what a few educators are willing to put out there in a public forum. Such a collection is in no way a complete gathering of concerns, but the words are powerful and should awaken decision-makers in education to raise the gates and let stakeholders in. Experts, teachers, parents, and students should have a much bigger say in the transformation, not the re-forming of an obsolete system.

What would students say in October, or how would parents weigh in while they sit around their kitchen tables trying to help with the gobs of assignments bearing down on their families? Recognizing that schools have become "less valued by students," notwithstanding how "mandated 'fixes'" demoralize teachers, Fullan and Rizzotto suggest that schooling becomes "more boring or alienating for the majority of students as they moved up the grade levels."[29] What can be done about it?

While schools do not have to be entertaining every minute of the day, educators can be inspired to make changes of the memory and meaning making kind. Examples do exist where educators have applied understandings of critical and creative thinking approaches through *Habits of Mind*, *New Pedagogies for Deep Learning*, and apprenticeship learning, for instance, that breathe life into project-based learning experiences.

Such engaging models of teaching and learning should not be adopted as paint-by-number prescriptions for replication; rather, they should function to inspire newcomers to become makers of customized learning plans and through the implementations of their constructions adapt and improve the curriculum on an ongoing basis. Such experiences are empowering, enriching, and professional. Closing the gates to professionalism by requiring educators to be on the same page at the same time using a set of lesson plans and units—written by others—is not a fix; it is a gate worthy of storming.

Given the volume of time students spend in schools, they should experience much more joy than they do. Easing up on the gates of expectations for students and teachers is a way forward. There is no need to make their experiences less rigorous, but paying deliberate attention to making their schooled world more meaningful would go a long way. Schools can be places where community members find joy and bring joy to others. We can do this! As Andy Hargreaves tweeted: "I see red, too, when teachers are being treated as badly as they are in NSW right now. Fight for the teachers who are fighting for the children."[30]

"You can't just walk away from your responsibilities because you made a mistake."

—Captain Kathryn Janeway

NOTES

1. M. Fullan & J. Rizzotto (2022), When it comes to the teacher shortage, who's abandoning whom?, https://michaelfullan.ca/wp-content/uploads/2022/10/When-It-Comes-to-the-Teacher-Shortage-copy.pdf.
2. A. Gavrielatos (2022, October 7). https://www.reddit.com/r/AustralianTeachers/comments/xxmhop/nsw_day_of_action_october_12th/.
3. M. Luther (2022, October 12), Twitter.
4. L. Deal [@lpdeal] (2022, October 12), Twitter.
5. W. Gassaway [@WendyGassaway] (2022, October 12), Twitter.
6. D. Cole (2022, October 12), Twitter.
7. A. Morbius (2022, October 12), Twitter.
8. C. Mann (2022, October 12), Twitter.
9. Ms.Carasco (2022, October 12), Twitter.
10. Kit (2022, October 12), Twitter.
11. W. Richards (2022, October 12), Twitter.
12. Jude (2002, October 13), Twitter.
13. J. Tutt (2022, October 13), Twitter.
14. S. Lynn (2022, October 13), Twitter.
15. G. McDermott (2022, October 13), Twitter.
16. K. Sullivan (2022, October 14), Twitter.
17. Patrick, Not Pat [@PresidentPat] (2022, October 14), Twitter.
18. Daily Maverick (2022, October 14), Twitter.
19. The Marigold Project (2022, October 14), Twitter.
20. S. Storey (2022, October 15), Twitter
21. M. Devlin (2022, October 15), Twitter.
22. L. Audrain (2022, October 15), Twitter.
23. A. Leung (2022, October 15), Twitter.
24. A. Gavrielatos (2022, October 16), Twitter.
25. north1963 [@north1963] (2022, October 16), Twitter.
26. M. Sanchez (2022, October 16), Twitter.
27. K. Arnold (2022, October 16), Twitter.
28. Mrs. Hernandez [@Mrs.Hernandez322] (2022, October 17), Twitter.

29. Fullan & Rizzotto, When it comes to the teacher shortage, who's abandoning whom?

30. A. Hargreaves (2022, October 12), Twitter.

Chapter 22

House of Mirrors

Barbara J. Smith

The lure of replication as a goal for schooling is much like operating within a house of mirrors. A narrow focus on standards, and assuming that schools should replicate what other schools with higher test scores do, discounts not only the complexity of schools, but the need for more engaging teaching and learning experiences.

The rush to build and multiply "the" ideal school may be based on good intentions, but plans to franchise private and private charter schools with corporate minds saving the day may indeed be arrogant, if not self-serving. With literally a century of research to apply, the assumption, for instance, that a charter school management company could determine which mirror is really "the" door in the pursuit of the most effective path for school improvement, is naïve on their part.

The thinking that all that is required to provide a quality education is a systematic implementation of policies and practices, ignores the reality that schools are dynamic cultures populated by human beings. Chomsky and Robichaud argue that "Standardized practices represent an attack on humanistic and critical education, as they are politically made to annihilate students and teacher's creativity, individuality, and autonomy to create more effective measures of uniformity and controls."[1]

According to Shafiyeva, from Azerbaijan:

My country, trying to improve the educational system, was trapped in the mechanism of standardized testing. This is one example that the countries trying to improve the system do not necessarily have to copy the West as the West has created its own problems on the way of advancement.The only positive outcome of the standardized test was that it had eliminated the corruption for university admission in Azerbaijan.[2]

A system of education should not hang in the balance of eliminating corruption. Creative and critical minds can come up with better ways to authenticate what students know.

If education was a matter of coloring in a stencil, how easy it would be to manage. The idea of a stenciled school implies that schools can be designed according to a fixed set of standards. How high the walls will be, what the capacity of each classroom can be, or how many offices a school is permitted is often set by regulations driven by efficiency and equity models. It sounds doable, but not so fast.

The people in each school are not the same; they are not widgets going about the business of teaching and learning. Tension arises when regulations are inflexible to a degree that it is impossible to design schools beyond the standard mold. The reckless appetite for the same meal could be a source of disengagement in today's schools. The people in each school need to be empowered to design their own schools, not simply operate a cookie-cutter system.

While some charter schools may house programs that support the kind of innovation that is worthy of a patent, many are drowning students and teachers in a sea of test preparation material, which dominates the curriculum. High student achievement, as measured by narrow standardized scores, often takes precedence over learning that supports success at college, in their careers, and in their lives. The peer-reviewed research that recommends improved and more informed practices with the child is left behind.

The charter school option in the United States has been a popular choice serving many inner-city communities. These schools using public funds, were granted more autonomy to explore new schooling approaches, presumably with less bureaucracy and more autonomy. The notion of self-governance, however, often stopped short of the people in the classrooms and their families. Small teams of under-qualified and, in most cases, non-educators who have never spent a day in a classroom teaching have been granted the power to design and re-form a highly controlled and outdated system of education.

Many of these charters were led by school trustees with minimal representation from the populations they served; many took guidance and mandated dated and unproven teaching and learning practices focused on student and teacher compliance. In Washington, DC, a single-page "Performance Management Framework" (PMF) was used as a dashboard designed to rank and compare schools for the purpose of having a built-in-system to determine which schools to close. And this framework is driving these decisions.

According to the DC Public Charter School Board, the following changes took place in charter schools over an eight-year period:

- Ten public charter LEAs had their charter revoked; three public charter LEAs were not renewed in their 15th year of operation.
- Six public charter LEAs relinquished their charter.
- Ten public charter campuses/programs closed or eliminated grades.
- Eight closed public charter LEAs were acquired by other operators.
- Eighteen public charter LEAs/programs closed because of academic deficiencies.
- Eight public charter LEAs/programs closed because of financial deficiencies/fiscal mismanagement.[3]

Heralded as evidence of rigor, this track record endorsed by the mayor, a questionable expert on education, requires upwards of thirty-five full-time people to manage the process.

Notably absent from the information about the PMF is a summary of funds collected for new school applications, nor the millions of tax dollars provided to former DCPSCB employees, now working for a local school "turnaround" consulting firm. When anyone indicates they have "cracked the code" on student achievement, it should be cause for concern. Furthermore, it seems appalling to use a tool, such as the PMF, that was not grounded in educational research. Such a weapon in the hands of individuals with little to no background in education, seems like it can only make a weak system worse, no matter how much money can be made.

With the newfound freedom and flexibility to generate new directions for education, charter schools, in many areas, have responded by developing a new system of bureaucracy, with even more gates sealed by even more red tape than many public systems. Rather than a surge of creative and engaging learning spaces, many charter schools are mere skeletons of innovation—incarcerating their communities to be compliant and "do as they are told."

When the word "innovation" is narrowly defined as technology, and reform efforts focus on returning to the "basics," it is doubtful that young people will be prepared for a world where critical and creative thinking action could lead to their success.

Gatekeeping exists in independent and international schools, as well. Like charter schools, most independent schools operate with a Board of Trustees overseeing the leadership and the budget of the school. Board members are not required to have education backgrounds, and therefore, trust the school leader to design the vision and direction for school improvement. Ideally, trustees, and in particular, the Board Chair, would act as partners to steer the school in a positive direction.

Given the absolute power of Board members, who can hire and ultimately fire a school leader, it makes sense that the makeup of such a membership include more individuals with a deep understanding of education. While trustees hold others accountable, it is less frequent that they would be held accountable, unless they vote each other out of the role.

Parents enroll their children in independent schools for many reasons, including lower class sizes and the long-standing reputation they may have in the community. Some may be legacy families who want their son or daughter to receive the same education they did. Many who can afford to pay a tuition for schooling may also be inclined to invest in donating to the school. People donate to what they know; while they may support new infrastructures in terms of upgrading physical spaces, donors rarely give funds for new directions and systematic change.

Independent schools are usually accredited by outside agencies that have explicit standards for school operations; many include expectations for governance and finance, which differs from public school reviews that focus mainly on the leadership and the teaching and learning in the classrooms. In addition to an independent school accreditation such as the National Association of Independent Schools (NAIS),[4] Council of International Schools (CIS),[5] the Canadian Accredited Independent School (CAIS),[6] and Middle States Accreditation (MSA),[7] some schools provide International Baccalaureate (IB)[8] accreditation, which overlays more specific academic standards. For each standard, there is an accepted way of operating, which can affirm practice at the same time as limiting innovation.

Many charters require schools to be accredited, in addition to participating in internal qualitative reviews conducted by their authorizers. What happens when the feedback from the accreditation documents is not congruent with the feedback from the authorizers? What qualifications do authorizers have to review schools? And how do authorizers know if the reviews are valid if they contract services from profit-making "turn around" companies, that recommend they be hired (after a convenient poor review) by a school to turn it around? This clearly lays out potential conflict of interest practices, yet such actions are commonplace in many charter systems in the United States.

According to Smith: "Educational research and rigor should not be sidestepped, ignored or rendered powerless in the challenge to grow charter schools into viable and respected institutions."[9] Based on experience as a charter school principal in Washington, DC, Smith claimed: "There appears to be a gap in terms of input from universities, into DC charter schools. Finding ways to bring in such expertise, could only strengthen the foundation of the current charter school offerings.[10] She added:

> it is in the best interest of young people to have a charter choice, that has an authorizer choice, and that it not be affiliated or controlled by the local school system. If the state or provincial governing body has approved charters than the

schools should ideally report to the state, where these officials can work with authorizers and accreditation agencies to ensure accountability.[11]

When authorizers or individuals in charge of schools have no knowledge or understanding of the work of school leadership experts such as Michael Fullan, Andy Hargreaves, or Ken Leithwood, this should raise some red flags. Furthermore, if authorizing teams, reviewers, or school leaders have not worked in classrooms, they cannot understand the complexity of a classroom or school.

School leaders and authorizers must have an understanding of pedagogically sound practices that include Habits of Mind, growth mindsets, multi-intelligences, sociocultural theory, Legitimate Peripheral Participation (LPP), Situated Learning, or the Zone of Proximal/Potential Development (ZPD). They should not be holding positions of added responsibility, and certainly not providing evidence that could close a school down. Without such depth and breadth of experience and knowledge, their lens for observing, examining, and analyzing would be severely limited. There should be no short cuts for educational leaders who skip the learning about the extensive body of reputable research in education.

International schools can also be independent schools, with trustees and accreditation gatekeepers, keeping schooling in a box. Those who color outside the lines of what understandings trustees know, or what standards are defined as "the" ideal practice, can stretch the limits for school improvement. Gatekeepers in these roles can act as managers, and when they do, the notion of change tends to be tolerated only in small chunks, disconnected from serious systematic improvement.

Selecting independent school trustees tends to be based on member recommendations or nominating committees made up of existing board members. Standards recommend that individuals who usually volunteer for such roles come from a variety of backgrounds to balance different kinds of needs and perspectives that can support the Board in their decision-making. The governance of any school can be more effective when they have people who can fill the need for expertise in real estate, law, maintenance, finance, marketing, and education.

Some Boards include parents who are not arms-length from the education of their students. The governance of independent schools tends not to be supportive of significant change.

It could be argued that a parent or teacher could add value to a Board of Governors, but even when they may claim they can separate their hats, it is possible to use their Board position to advance their child and their work, over others. No question, these key stakeholders have skin in the game, and their voices should be heard.

A school leader needs to have a pulse on the community and provide ample opportunity for parents, teachers, and students to weigh in on matters related to the school. Making the responses to annual surveys transparent and forming action committees to address school improvement needs would be better options for parent and teacher involvement in school affairs.

Private schools operate within a different leadership structure. The owner or group of investors who have financial stakes in the school make key decisions. There are no Boards of Directors and they may not have bylaws, but like all organizations, they must operate within the scope of the law. Many charter schools are privately owned, and as such are driven by the profit motive. Given such schools do not receive government funding, nor answer to a Board of Directors, their financial statements and budgets are not privy to scrutinized examinations by elected officials or professional auditors. The owners are free to profit from their tuitions.

Often independent schools are lumped in with private schools, but the oversight is very different. Funds raised in nonprofit independent schools go back into the school, whereas the profits made in private schools have every legal right to be distributed amongst the owners. Many charter school management companies create a school framework and replicate it in as many communities and states as they can. Peter Greene noted, "charter school operators have long worked a variety of loopholes, keeping the sector a highly profitable one, and most of those loopholes involve a non-profit charter school hiring a for-profit business."[12] The Biden administration promised to put a stop to funding not-for-profit charter schools who hand over their operations to for-profit charter companies.

The "canning" of education can happen in for-profit and non-for-profit organizations. The IB program in a popular non-profit foundation that influences schools around the globe. They determine many parameters such as assessment and mandatory courses that define their brand. Schools that meet their standards can apply for accreditation.

The lure of replicating schools and standards can seemingly make things easier and more efficient, but the implementation of what works for one school can never be assumed as what will work well in another. If the metrics for comparing schools is whittled down to a narrow view of test results, then marketers may wish to claim that one approach is better than others.

When students returned after COVID, there was an apparent uptake in disciplinary problems in schools. While it was a distraction to blame poor behavior on the parents, as lax disciplinarians, there has been little attention paid to what schools can control, and that is a boring curriculum that teachers are mandated to "deliver."

An insightful tweet shared by James Ladwig noted: "The challenges faced by kids after school closures isn't so much what they missed, it's being forced back into a system they know doesn't and didn't serve them well in the first place."[13] The design of quiet halls and the rigid "no talking" classrooms in charter schools, seems to reflect a haunting awareness that unless these schools run a tight ship, no student or teacher would be interested in the program. Do parents really want their children to be compliant—or do they want them to learn and enjoy learning?

It would be an oxymoron to place teacher-directed and creative classrooms in the same goal statement. Schools that commit to do both are operating in a house of mirrors, pretending to be everything at the same time, by promoting opposing goals. Creativity and cloning are opposites, and as such should be debated using evidence and research for solid grounding.

If schools are spaces where students are educated to think critically and creatively, then what happens in the school and how the school is designed need to be open for innovation.

The idea that a great school can be scaled and replicated assumes a fixed view of education, as if "the" utopian school exists. The lure of replication may seem like a worthy goal, but there is no proven right way of operating schools; rather, schools must evolve as a culture grows and changes with time. The research in education is clear that schooling should not support a one-size-fits-all approach to teaching and learning, so how can there be a place for talk of franchising and duplicating school operations, programs, budgets, and physical plants?

The framing of schools and the cloning of such blueprints are gatekeeping actions that serve to safeguard against school improvement efforts. Reform is often misunderstood as change by itself, but the word means to re-formulate what already exists. Rather than reforming or re-inventing, efforts at school improvement should be focused on transformation via innovation. If schools do not serve all students well, then a significant change is necessary, not a repositioning of the same chairs that are already comfortable for high performing students.

It's an unwise practice to think about scaling schools; the conjecture that what is to be replicated is of most worth is indeed an erroneous assumption, no matter what the lure of projected cost savings might be. Schools should not be formulated by stencils, framed and bound by a gatekeeping precision of a recipe book. It's time to decommission the empty mirrors, void of substance, and support a clear path to school innovation and change.

> *"We're to put back into spacedock immediately to be decommissioned."*
> —Communications Officer Uhura

NOTES

1. A. Robichaud & N. Chomsky (2014), Interview with Noam Chomsky on education, *Radical Pedagogy*, *11*(1).
2. U. Shafiyeva (2021, August), Literacy and standardized testing, *Literacy Letters*, p. 1.
3. DC Public Charter School Board. https://dcpcsb.org.
4. National Association of Independent Schools (NAIS), https://www.nais.org.
5. Council of International Schools (CIS), https://www.cois.org/
6. Canadian Accredited Independent School (CAIS), https://www.cais.ca.
7. Middle States Accreditation (MSA), https://www.msa-cess.org.
8. International Baccalaureate (IB), https://www.ibo.org.
9. B. J. Smith (2017), *A charter school principal's story: A view from the inside*, p. 281.
10. Smith, *A charter school principal's story*, pp. 275–276.
11. Smith, *A charter school principal's story*, p. 275.
12. P. Greene (2021, July 21), What's the matter with for profit charter school management?, *Forbes*, https://www.forbes.com/sites/petergreene/2021/07/21/whats-the-matter-with-for-profit-charter-school-management/?sh=2d1d7bc77a3e.
13. L. Ladwig (2022, October 20), Twitter.

Chapter 23

Saving Students from a Shattered System

Eldon "Cap" Lee

Brown vs Board of Education clearly disallowed school segregation at any level in the United States. "The Kansas case was unique . . . that there was no contention of gross inferiority of the segregated schools' physical plant, curriculum, or staff."[1] This clearly rejects any exception to the rule under any conditions. However, what it does not consider is the equality of preparation necessary for students to be successful, not only on a pathway to a university, but a pathway for daily living beyond the four walls of the school. We must recognize that students need to attend a school that is much more than a shattered "house of mirrors."

Hidden in the depths of the current system and philosophy of education is the lack of equality created by a lack of understanding that all students are different and perform in different ways. I call this the EQUALITY OF DIFFERENTIATION. As the microscope focuses on individual students, the system is designed to see all through a blurred lens. Why isn't every child in the same place at the same time taking the same standardized test? In reference to the movie Stepford Wives, we do not have "Stepford Kids"[2] as in the movie. Can you imagine what life would be like under those conditions?

Those conditions will never exist in our lifetime and hopefully will never, ever exist. In an academic sense, students will never have the same ability to take a standardized test, or invent a new mouse trap or overcome failure, or graduate after four years. This is clear with the wide range of those with special learning needs as well as those in general education and even gifted programs.

When considering equity, we only need to look at the recent pandemic for the answer. The amount of time that students were confined to their homes, away from in- school learning, was devastating to their education. It soon became clear that with skill levels now all over the board, those students would not return to school fitting into the one-size-fits-all education curriculum currently available.[3]

Questions that arose without answers in the current system are: What grade are the students in? Are they promoted without learning? Are they retained into oblivion taking the first steps to the school to prison pipeline? Will they be excluded by an SAT or other standardized test designed to, in the words of Thomas Jefferson, "rake a few geniuses from the rubbish"?

The lessons of the pandemic are clear. The system is not working for those students, and never will. It was never designed to serve all students. What is clear to some, but not clear to many, is the system has never worked for some Black and Brown as well as occasional white students for the last two hundred years. The systemic goal of education is to maintain the subclass by ALLOWING roadblocks to learning to be systematically placed in front of unwitting students.

Learning is slowed by childhood stress, malnutrition, lead in the water, and a host of other issues especially including a "failure system" that is designed to push kids out of school. Once behind, the current system makes it nearly impossible for students to catch up and graduate on the same day at the same time as the "accepted" norm.

It is important to understand that all Black and Brown students are not subject to these roadblocks. In fact many, if not most, are protected from those roadblocks and will do well under most circumstances. However, when students enter a classroom, no teacher knows which students have faced roadblocks and which haven't. That is why all students must be met with high expectations to allow those skilled Black and Brown students to advance to their fullest potential regardless of the assessment methods.

This discussion is not about why students can or can't be successful under the current admission system; it's about the real way students can demonstrate the skills needed to move forward to their pathway to success. Real demonstrations of learning will be documented to indicate their real skills. Letter grades and the test are artificial and therefore must be excluded from the process.

Solutions are available if only we could get around the massive roadblocks put in the way of educators. The reality is that corporate leadership and pandering politicians demand the status quo by simply blaming the teachers. The Pete Seeger song "Where's the Trouble at the Bottom?" points out the confusion that exists trying to fix a failed system of education. Those who are pushed out of the system are acceptable to the corporations and politicians, and, as an added bonus, it saves them money in their education budget. Of course, the prison budget is another story.

What if, as a solution, students developed a portfolio throughout their final four years of secondary school? And this portfolio was presented to the University Admission Department without meaningless letter grades and test scores. And that portfolio was scrutinized by a team of professors, social workers, and others. Think of the possibilities. The results could be a completely different approach to university or college admittance.

Consider this: A student is accepted and admitted to a university with a specific focus as determined by their portfolio and the passion of the student. Or, they are not accepted at this time but when they increase their skills in well- defined, specific areas, their application will be reviewed. Community colleges would then be seen as an extension of high school, a stepping stone to a university and/or preparation for a career of one's choosing. Most are already proficient in those roles, however under this plan, there would be specific learning goals for specific students.

Of utmost importance is, unlike letter grades and a standardized test, the portfolio would allow students to access their background information. This demands the complete acceptance of cultural differences. When this becomes the norm, an even playing field would be available with guidance from *Brown vs Board of Education*. The law would then demand fair integration on all levels and take away excuses of PERCEIVED lack of abilities determined by an artificial test, fake grade point averages, and any school discrimination. ANY DISCRIMINATION WOULD BE LOUD, CLEAR, AND INEXCUSABLE! The EQUALITY OF DIFFERENTIATION would take every child to their maximum potential!

NOTES

Eldon "Cap" Lee, Adapted with permission from http://savingstudents-caplee.blogspot.com/2022/10/brown-vs-board.html?m=1.

1. Brown Vs Board of Education: Solidified (update, 10/21), https://en.m.wikipedia.org/wiki/Brown_v._Board_of_Education.

2. Stepford Wives, https://en.wikipedia.org/wiki/The_Stepford_Wives.

3. Lee, Eldon "Cap," *A failed system: Pandemic related solutions to a 200-year-old education.*

Chapter 24

The Sausage Machine
Policy Making and School Funding

Barbara J. Smith

The "head office" in any organization can satirically be referred to as a sausage machine. This tends to be places in school district or state/provincial or national offices where the management of schools meets the needs of schools, where both meet the reality of the budget. People in schools are not sausages, and to ensure that they have what they need to support and experience a high-quality education, the leaders in head offices need to recognize that schools are not machines, nor should all students be filtered through the same grinder.

When school administrators or teachers flip through a school handbook to clarify policy, they are often checking for protocols related to school discipline. It was popular at one time to implement "zero tolerance" policies to make expulsion an automatic consequence when students had committed serious offenses such as violent acts toward community members. Decades later, there are still community members who support such policies. According to Vern Hughes, Director of the Civil Society in Australia:

> All public schools should have the right to expel disruptive or poorly behaving students. The state school system has an obligation to accommodate disruptive and poorly behaving students in intensive support settings until they are able to resume participation in mainstream schools. The state school system also has an obligation to prevent disruptive or poorly performing students from impeding the development of other students.[1]

Such positions shortcut the need to explore the complexity of each situation, almost pronouncing guilt prior to a trial, certainly not modelling democratic ideals.

Policies are established to protect the students and staff as well as the school itself. Even when lawyers provide elaborate language to protect the school from harm, a policy is never foolproof. While policies remain legal entities, members of the school community should never assume that they are fixed in time.

The COVID pandemic brought in a tsunami of protocols that were revised on a regular basis, in keeping with new ongoing scientific findings. Detailing whether students and families on school campuses must wear masks, how far apart community members must be, and the implementing of robust cleaning protocols were only a few items in multi-page documents that needed to be developed in record breaking time.

Schools systems are highly engineered and complex, but that doesn't mean their structures cannot be altered. The original design of any institution should be flexible enough to permit and embrace ongoing improvement.

The silos in school districts and governmental structures function more in a managerial mode, rather than a conduit for inspiring, mentoring, or leadership growth. The sausage machine could be more than a grinding machine for policies. The relationships with such authorities can be somewhat automated and regimented. Educators can contact officials by leaving emails or phone messages, and while responses may happen in a timely manner, sausage makers rarely arouse an emotional connection. Such interactions can come across as transactional.

How school authorities respond to stakeholders exposes what is valued by such power brokers in education. Depending on the individuals in these head office roles, the responses can be somewhat detached, automated, and scripted. The policy of treating everyone equitably seems to reflect a system that endorses a transactional approach to education, rather than transformational experiences. Transactions are never equal; the individuals in positions of power tend to transmit policy, rather than commit to changing it.

When the critical mass of educators hired in head office positions at the district, state, provincial, or national level focus on implementing programs that support existing policies, then these offices tend to behave in a more managerial or transactional way. System improvement, however, cannot happen in isolation of a transformational culture.

Even when experts claim that change must be mobilized by classroom teachers, it is difficult for teachers to make improvements within confined school policies. Teachers in public systems are expected to implement initiatives that support governmental or district directives, with the hope they will ultimately transform students, teachers, and schools. The mismatch, however, occurs when implementors are expected to adopt recommendations. It is commonplace for teachers to be the deliverers of curriculum designed by others who are not familiar with the uniqueness of each classroom.

Policies exist to support differentiated practices, but the emphasis on standards for each grade and the value placed on high stakes testing seem to take precedence over all over activity.

Kevin Bartlett, Founding Director of The Common Ground Collaborative, claimed: "The 'standards' are imposed on teachers, not developed with them . . . so the systems have little credibility."[2]

All roads lead back to a mechanized system of curriculum delivery, giving schools and districts options to present them in connected ways through project-based learning initiatives. While this sounds promising for engaging and empowering teachers and students, there are few time provisions afforded in a teacher's schedule for the design and customization of more innovative practices. As Sheninger noted: "Rigid school schedules and archaic policies should not dictate the types of learning experiences students should have available for them today."[3]

Policies aimed at promoting the development of humanity are compartmentalized; social and emotional learning are featured as checklists on a report card, leading readers to surmise that learning and thinking skills have lesser importance. People have multiple intelligences, not separate from one another. Yet schools are organized into arbitrary subjects disconnected from each other. According to Jack Miller,

> all of this impetus on testing and standardized testing has got to be changed. We need accountability but we do not need a system which creates so much fear, which is basically what the standardized testing movement does. For whatever it is supposed to achieve, the negatives far outweigh any of the positive elements. Finland is an example of a country that has an exceptional education system that doesn't focus on these kinds of tests.[4]

Referring to the Ontario Ministry of Education, Miller added,

> The problem in our school system . . . is that it is very much focused on individual competition which reinforces a sense of separation rather than compassion. I think one of the major efforts in education should be to move to where compassion, forgiveness and empathy become central aspects of education.[5]

The importance of happiness and social and emotional development in schools is under-rated. Even in the response to wellness needs during and following the COVID pandemic, actions taken tended to be ones that fit within the current system of school operations.

Viewing school policies from a holistic perspective, rather than fragmented parts of a system, is necessary when designing and revising strategic plans. Benjamin Freud recognized that the future is plural; there are many options and possibilities:

> the futures of education are tied to the futures of the system, the futures of society, the futures of life. Education can never be silo'd or isolated as if it existed on its own. And it's not about adding on "what competencies do we need for the workplace of tomorrow?"[6]

The volume of school policies can be as complicated as tax laws; the legal system can entrench how school systems address many aspects of an organization's structure including the distribution of time, the curriculum, disciplinary procedures, and staffing. While laws are meant to protect individuals, they can also deter school improvement.

DISTRIBUTION OF TIME

Time is one of the most controlled elements in schools. It may seem like a principal and staff would have a say in how time is carved up for teaching, learning, and professional growth, but school leaders with their boots on the ground must abide by policy or seek permission for changes from officials deep in district or state offices.

Frustrated by the limited autonomy at the school level, Pasi Sahlberg noted: "they always have to ask permission from somebody to make simple changes like giving children more recess time," adding, "it's much more about waiting for this central office in the state to tell the schools what to do."[7] Why do school leaders need ways to consult the school system's publicist, in order to make decisions about how best to structure time in schools?

Schools are mandated to admit and dismiss students based on a standard number of minutes per day. Stakeholders in one particular public school do not have the authority to start school at a later time, even if the research supports it. Stephen Braybrook recommended starting the school day at 10 a.m.:

> Research by an OU academic has found that children between the ages of 13–16 who started their school day at 10am, had improved health (as measured by number of sick days) by over 50% and a 12% on better grades. I suggest this would also be the same for ages 12–19. This directly links to looking at blue screens past 11pm lowers dopamine levels and increases the feeling of depression. So many students spend time on their phones past 11, no wondering what they struggle to start the learning day at 8.30/9am.[8]

The desperate rush to fill content gaps has many schools gaining special permission to lengthen the school day or the school year. Charter, independent, and private schools have more autonomy to make such changes. Rather than reducing the amount of time in school, as research suggests, they often join the bandwagon to add more instruction to the day, assuming it will magically restore the learning loss.

In the United States, the worshipping of the Carnegie Credit with the minutes defined for a course of study is centrally controlled at the state level. Carving courses up into micro-credentials that might collectively meet the timed requirements of a credit is not permitted. A biology course in grade 12 must be completed in so many consecutive minutes in one school year; even if it were spread out over two years for deeper learning, educators are not allowed to tinker with such historically defined formulas.

Policies exist in some school districts about when sick days can be taken and when staff can take part in professional learning. Teachers may not sign up for conferences happening in the final week of school; teachers may not be permitted to meet after school for workshops or to collaborate on committees. In some cases, the time limits are imposed by the employers and in other cases, they can be built into extensive employment agreements.

The head office employees can be quite expert at creating bureaucracy. Some school boards do not permit employees to participate in professional learning outside their school or community. Some may support teachers attending conferences in other jurisdictions or countries if they have been selected as presenters, but this is rare.

Some school boards even vote on operational decisions such as the time limits for parent-teacher conferences that are mandated at least twice a year. The limited time afforded for middle and high school parents to have access to each of their child's teachers is a chronic problem. Even though three to five minutes is not enough time to form a relationship, communicate achievement, and set up action plans for next steps, the technology world has engineered pristine software programs to coordinate such visits within the confines of usually a day and half investment of overall time.

Many gatekeepers do not see beyond the current limitations of teacher conferences. Efforts for improvement are often dedicated to fine tuning this weak practice, rather than look for increasing time for such important communication. It makes sense that making more afterwork hours available, at the same time as giving teachers the same time off during the school day might be one option for improving the use of such potentially interactive time.

A gatekeeper might shut down the idea arguing that students still need to be supervised at school during the day when families are at work. The coordination of several days of elective programming from specialists in the community (i.e., chess, robotics, theatre . . .) could give teachers time to arrive much later in the day to make up for working after hours on multiple days set aside for parent-teacher conferencing. Managers find reasons why something can't be done; leaders find a way to make improvement happen.

Managers see scheduling as choosing to have block scheduling, or not. Even though students need extended time for deep learning, there are few schools that use semesters or modified forms of "semestering." There are significant drawbacks to using schedules that give students a workload in excess of six classes in one term. Teachers would never accept a teaching load of many different subject areas, yet schools impose such a fragmented learning experience on students.

Pacing guides are oxymorons. When calendars are used to pitch the teaching of different groups of students at the same place at the same time, the hypocrisy of a differentiated program is revealed. A "guide" is what teachers should use to plan their own units, but it should not be a tool for comparing how fast students in one class versus another can cover a curriculum. Once again, software programs have been created to populate a frenzy of content that teachers must enter to build out "when" content should be introduced in stuffed to the brim digital pacing guides.

ACADEMIC POLICIES

Douglas Reeves makes a powerful point after many states paused annual testing during the pandemic:

> While many states suspended annual testing guides, there has been no reduction of the expectations that teachers cover all grade-level standards. That was preposterous before the pandemic and remains doubly today. It leaves teachers in an impossible position, attempting to engage in frantic and fragmented "delivery" of content rather than focused learning experiences. School leaders also face the temptation of fragmentation, as federal funds associated with pandemic relief have frequently been used to purchase one program after another. This leaves schools buried under the weight of initiative fatigue.[9]

With so much content clogging the curriculum of each discipline, there is little room for piloting new courses, inter-disciplinary experiences, and engaging and memory-making learning experiences of the apprenticeship kind. The volume of curriculum crammed into different grades functions as a gatekeeper limiting innovative learning experiences.

Following the state, provincial, or national curriculum is policy that dictates the "same" program for all. Furthermore, schools are not permitted to design report cards that are customized to fit innovative programs; is it because such programs are not fitting in the same box?

School policies should be congruent with each other. How can schools commit and implement differentiated learning policies at the same time as expect students to learn content at the same pace and be tested at the same time?

The investment in textbooks puts pressure on teachers to plan for their use, rather than creating new teaching and learning resources. School leaders, and teachers, so jammed with busy work, must trust the table of contents in a textbook as the curriculum. Hughes claimed:

> Every teacher is entitled to a portable, online Core Curriculum Teaching Plan that specifies year and stage-specific core knowledge requirements, teaching methodologies, and teaching resources. Teachers should not be expected to have to devise plans for every subject and every student.[10]

It's one thing for a noneducator to share such a view but when those responsible for education support similar views, the quality of educational leadership should come into question. In New South Wales, Australia, government officials have responded to the teacher's lack of time by provided canned lessons as a "helping hand."

> The state's education minister Sarah Mitchell announced teachers will be given curriculum lesson plans, texts and learning materials to ease the pressure on their workloads. This will come via a "bank" of "high-quality, sequenced curriculum resources." Mitchell said this "game changer" has been developed off the back of teachers' concerns.[11]

Policies that promote canned programs are not game changers. By giving teachers a handout rather than a hand-up, it is doubtful they would feel any sense of ownership, empowerment, or engagement. Policies that support hiring more teachers to give them more time to design their own lessons and materials makes more sense if building a professional culture matters. As Wilson and McGrath-Champ from the University of Sydney, suggest: "This is like banging our heads against the wall . . . outsourcing lesson planning has NSW teachers hopping mad."[12]

PEOPLE POLICIES

Schools have many policies that relate to people and how people in schools relate to each other. During the COVID crisis, parents were no longer permitted to enter many schools; staff meetings were disbanded or discouraged;

cooperative paired or group work could only happen in a virtual setting. Policies for interactions at schools changed overnight in order to ensure safe learning spaces.

The ideal size of a classroom is the source of debate within schools and outside institutions. While it may make economic sense to have twenty or more students in a classroom, it is not an ideal condition for teaching and learning. When schools were locked down during the pandemic and had to move to Zoom or other virtual portals, it became strikingly evident that a teacher with fewer student screens to manage in a digital classroom was more effective.

The concern for "learning loss," which some governments believe is a Band-Aid tutoring voucher will solve, was not needed when schools were already managing with class sizes of eight to twelve students. A screenshot of a classroom with so many students that the arrow needed to be pressed to check if they were all present—represents a chilling reminder that there are too many students plopped in classrooms every day, enough to build up a healthy disenfranchised community of students who do not fit in, or bother being engaged in study.

Why is it that in the corporate world they tend to work with smaller ratios of supervisor to employee reporting scenarios? As Smith noted: "Quality control is at risk when leaders or supervisors are stretched too thin."[13] Many businesses use an 8:1 ratio that enables bosses to not only appraise their direct reports, but support and mentor them. Such a culture thrives on increasing the layers of leadership opportunities, while providing effective ongoing learning conditions within an organization. It is incomprehensible that something as important as teaching and learning in a school setting would have anything less than what many adults embrace in their working environments.

It seems that interactions outside of school pay more attention to effective instructional ratios. At camp, a counselor rarely has more than eight campers to care for; if there are more young people added to the tent or cabin, they would have a CIT or counsellor-in-training assigned to their unit. Imagine if there were twenty non-swimmers in a pool with a swim instructor at the same time? Not only would this be unsafe, but it would also be like herding cats. How many scouts are there in a troop and what are the leader to scout ratios?

Why is there such a growing demand for tutors to supplement, or some might say, carry the load of an education? It is impossible to provide personalized, individualized, or customized learning, in other words, a quality education, for students when the teacher:student ratios are so high. When a teacher has more time to support students, more learning can happen.

Schools should not be shortchanged, nor should decision makers in education attach themselves to research that indicates class size doesn't matter. It does matter; more in-depth examination of Dewey, Vygotsky, and the messages of more modern curriculum experts could never argue that increasing the number of students in a class is better. Fewer students increase the opportunity for talking with an expert, to become like an expert. Teaching and learning should be about apprenticing and moving from novice to more expert understandings.

There are schools who lump all staff members into their overall average ratios, but this data can be misleading. If the school leaders were picking up classes, then it would be fair to include them in such a calculation. But doing rounds and popping in every once in a while is not teaching. Not only are there too many students in classrooms for a single teacher to teach, but there are also too many teachers for a school principal to support and appraise with much hope of success.

How schools are organized should be based on what is best for the students. Class size should not have to be a demand in contract negotiations. It should already be implemented by the experts responsible for implementing school budgets. The old formulas do not suffice; to fund the salaries for more teachers, the budgets not only need to be re-purposed, but there is a need for a larger allotment of funds, to right this keeling ship.

The efforts by many entrepreneurs to save education by creating charter schools in the United States has been generally unsuccessful. Many took the shortcut around the body of educational research that could have informed how to better invest their funds. By ignoring a powerful 8:1 direct report ratio used in their own business cultures, many charters missed an opportunity to support significant school change. As Smith noted:

> Rather than taking the time and putting in the hard work to help people re-shape and improve their school cultures, many so-called "experts" try to fast-track short-term results to prove that charter schools are better options. Given that human capital carves up so much of the school budget, it makes sense to look beyond the quick fixes to how restructuring can save schools money and re-direct expenses, so they have a direct impact on students and staff development.[14]

If donors took a few courses in teaching and learning, they might have been aware of more effective paths for change. By funding unproven practices such as promoting unqualified school leaders and creating an overcrowded curriculum only to cram it down students' throats for the purpose of testing, seemed to only provide gains, often substantial ones, for people outside of the field of education. It seems that those waving the flag of accountability were not so willing to be held accountable for the mess made as a result of wasted funding and skipping the need for an education about education.

It takes more ingenuity to create new education institutions than it does to re-package the existing ship with the benefit of getting to choose from a cloned army of schools. What's the point in having policies about school choice when the schools that are permitted to stay open must be replicates of each other? Choice, if there are real options, would not be a bad thing. It is satirical, however, that the "choice" policy, and the capacity to be better than other schools, using questionable standardized tests, is presented as the Holy Grail, rather than the engagement of students and teachers in schools.

To get to policies that can support significant change in school, it is important to consider the power that labor laws in various states and countries hold over the process of change. For schools to re-structure, this usually means that employees will need to take on different roles, and the degree to which staff members may be asked to change can be a legal matter. Without the blessing of each employee, the opportunity to improve with change can be shut down. Schools are vulnerable to legal action, which can take up enormous amounts of human energy.

In many areas of the world, the teacher contracts, once accepted, mean that staff members have a right to work under those conditions for the remainder of their careers. This means that what they do, in the time frames that they enter in, are similar to a tenured position, and such positions, based on legal policy, are set for life. This can make school improvement a disenchanted dream. For significant change to happen in any kind of school setting, there needs to be more flexibility in labor laws, as many exist today.

Even though teachers may want to work with smaller class sizes, with hours of planning time per day, making such changes happen is near to impossible as their agreements bind them to a decaying education system. Striking action about pay and conditions involves the design of new layers of policies within various education unions or associations. Teachers, for instance, may not be permitted to provide supervision for extra-curricular activities; non-instructional employees are committed to participating in protests to support teacher contract negotiations, and vice versa.

Even when teachers have the Minister of Labor on speed dial, they may not realize that this protection is also a quarantine condition against change. Rarely do employees strike to change the system, but educated leaders in a system are bound by the legal contracts of its employees, so school leaders rarely can make an impact, relinquishing to the same hand-cuffed existence year after year.

FACILITY FORMULAS

Schools are not banquet halls, and their occupancy rates should not be based on fire regulations. While they must adhere to laws and regulations it should not mean that the sizes of schools and the number of students should be based on such maximums. There is more to fit in a classroom in the twenty-first century. No matter how small we can make technology, it requires real estate in the classroom to be effective. In the past, students had to wait to log in until they were scheduled in computer labs, but today students need ongoing access to technology, and space in classrooms needs to be dedicated for storage and recharging.

Furthermore, classrooms need space to honor the work of students, and repurposing rooms to be more like learning labs is more conducive to ideal learning conditions. Reducing the number of students in classrooms should not mean that the existing classroom sizes are too large. Space is needed.

Policies surrounding the ideal school and classroom sizes should be aligned with ideal practices of teaching and learning. Fewer students in a school increases the opportunities for students to be included and feel a part of a community. If a principal cannot name every student and ideally every parent within the first three months of school, then the physical plant is more of a holding tank than a community. School leaders have little choice in large industrial modelled schools that house upward of over three hundred students to rely on others to know designated chunks of students, and this is anything but ideal.

Who is inquiring into the effectiveness of the design and capacity of school facilities? And based on such study, what ideal conditions are being recommended in the form of new, brave policies for operating schools in a district, state/province, or country? The extensive research on the value of small schools has existed for decades, but it seems like parents looking for alternatives to the "superschools" that often house thousands of students, have created a demand for smaller micro-schools.

Changing the same old mold for schools can happen, without a huge outpouring of additional costs. While it makes sense for school systems to distribute funds fairly to provide equitable services and support, an absolute goal of replicating educational institutions can be cause for concern. Funding formulas can wipe away distinct school identities in a heartbeat. School values grounded in educational research should drive the school budget, not the other way around.

In *How Much Does a Great School Cost? School Economies and School Values*, Smith claims: "Schools are complex institutions and as such require much more than simply funding formulas to guide their operation."[15] The lure of technology may seem like a quick fix to catapult schools into the twenty-first century, but the over-reliance and investment in digital tools and options should not exist as isolated strategies separate from or in the place of curriculum innovation.

According to Justin Reich, Director of the MIT Teaching Lab:

Proponents of large-scale learning have boldly promised that technology can disrupt traditional approaches to schooling, radically accelerating learning and democratizing education. Much-publicized experiments, often underwritten by Silicon Valley entrepreneurs, have been launched at elite universities and in elementary schools in the poorest neighborhoods.[16]

In his book, *Failure to Disrupt: Why Technology Alone Can't Transform Education*, he claims that "our learning technologies are only as strong as the communities of educators that guide their use"[17] (ix).

While students need experts to guide them in person or digitally, it is surprising how attendance policies seem to be accepted without question, as a data source for assessing quality. The pandemic created a scenario in which sitting in school desks was not necessary. Students may have been present on screens, but when they were able to stop the video, how would anyone know if they were there? The lockdown should have made more policymakers or maintainers cognizant of the fact that evidence of learning is more significant than an attendance score.

There is no doubt about the advantages of face-to-face learning, but minutes of counting seats in desks should be the target of further challenge. Funding formulas should not be tied to student attendance in schools, nor should credits be achieved because students spend the entire term or year in the teacher's sights for an exact period of time. How is it that policymakers can be so arrogant to not accept the very real fact that students can learn in a variety of settings, and that learning spaces can happen outside the brick and mortar of a school building?

Attendance data is easy to gather, but it is not evidence of learning. Creating under-researched and overly engineered dashboard tools that equate attendance with achievement is non-sensical, yet the development of matrices that include attendance metrics, is often prepared for by lay people to sway their support for a fixed model of education. As Daniel Buck tweeted: "If a student has mastered basic literacy, numeracy, science, and civics, I see no reason why the state compels them into school attendance until they're 16–18."[18]

Rick Lewis posted on The Principal's Desk about his experiences at an international IB School in Austria:

> My school doesn't count or track tardies, we have no dress code, we have recess/break for all grades (students have an hour for lunch and break), we have a mid-morning snack break (15 minutes), we are against homework, there's no phone policy (students have them all day), all our teachers have a day off (work four days), we treat our HS students like adults . . . and we don't do detentions. Our results are above the world average, so it must work. 100% acceptance rate to universities for our graduates. It's possible to run a school without all these blinders. We focus on teaching and learning. The other stuff is just clutter. Not

trying to offend anyone, just saying it's possible to run a school without all these things.[19]

Many policies pressed out by school systems can function as gatekeepers that can bind and clutter up an education.

If schools operated with fewer policies, they would require fewer managers to monitor them, and perhaps these bodies, in new positions, could add to the teaching force to reduce the teacher:student ratio; it's a radical thought to think about the possibilities of changing staffing to improve schools. It's not enough to change our principals; careful thought should go into how all stakeholders can do things differently, if they really want to improve schools. Solly Khan, from the Guardian Institute in South Africa suggested that it is a "sad reality" that is the antithesis of Dewey's intention noting: "This is no fault of the teacher as the education system upon which it was built on since time immemorial frowns on and punishes anyone who dares to speak out or deviate from the norm."[20]

Sheninger suggests that a "culture shock" is required, one that embraces failure as a part of learning. He further noted: "The fear of failure has become the main driver of instructional practices that maintain conformity, control and the status quo. Thus an innovative school culture that students and educators yearn for becomes a pipe dream at best."[21]

STRATEGIC AND SCHOOL IMPROVEMENT PLANNING

Strategic planning and school improvement planning can be viewed as separate assignments; they can be linked, but both may not be necessary. Strategic plans can be a long-term document that functions as a gauge for what is to be emphasized in three-, five-, or even ten-year chunks. Ideally, a strategic plan will highlight new initiatives that require concerted effort to implement, adapt, and revise. Stakeholders need to give new initiatives at least a three-year time frame to adequately assess their value.

There are two versions of a strategic plan: one that should be based on ideas and actions and one that itemizes the cost of the ideas and actions over time. Often the documents that include the financing of change are kept within the confines of a board; rarely are such budgets strategic or transparent. When a school or district embraces a "what's next" mindset, the stakeholders are committed to growing and improving. In such a culture, the school improvement plan and the strategic plan are one and the same; there is no need to write separate documents that recommend the same actions.

New schools or schools targeted to design and implement innovative practices should not be held accountable by the same tools that rank schools committed to fixed programs. Implementing a strategic or school improvement plan for transforming a school requires at least three years without the disruption of testing, to permit new practices to take hold and thrive in a new culture. Testing and gathering benchmark data at the beginning or throughout the process can only compromise the work of a transforming team, fueled by growth mindsets. Standardized tests are for standardized schools led by managers with fixed mindsets, programs, and policies.

It does not make sense to put energy into ten-year plans; even five-year plans seem to be too far into the future to make reliable predictions. It is not uncommon for accreditation reviewers to ask for ten-year budget projections, but if the school is committed to change, new patterns of funding projections should emerge as new initiatives are implemented. Some schools may have ten-year plans, or more leases, or large capital expenses targeted for major renovations; in such cases, it makes sense for schools to outline lengthier plans to ensure they will have the funds to cover the costs along the way.

While plans should be detailed, they should not be so fixed that in their implementation, there is no room for adjustments or adaptations as they unfold. Funding for certain line items on a budget would be used to fund new initiatives, which in turn create new line items. The need to view trends in budgets over time can make the inclusion of additional line-items more complicated for accountants and auditors.

Budgets with line items that mirror other schools, or do not change over time, are more symptomatic of schools operating within management systems. School leaders who are committed to ongoing school improvement in transformation-focused schools will need to work with trustees and trailblazing bookkeepers who have growth mindsets, people who can see the budget as a reflection of school values, not a template borrowed or mandated from another school.

According to Smith:

> The phrase—"we do not need to re-invent the wheel" is often echoed by forces that preserve the status quo. The notion of innovation fitting into an existing budget means that new ideas must compete with older ways of doing school. For fresh ideas to take shape, we must embrace the idea of a new wheel and a new path down a road not taken. Such a path can be risky for the status funding quo. The autopsies of the *"walking dead"* reforms in education reveal much about good plans, that were poorly implemented, or naive plans void of big picture alignment.[22]

She added, "Budgets . . . do not need to be fixed; rather, there are ample ways to revise spending to adjust for new or changing values in a school."[23] The need for school change is at odds with the standards that support fixed systems.

According to Owen: "Maybe the pandemic would be a catalyst for educators, students, parents, and community members to come together, on behalf of children, and totally rethink education and how we could better serve all children."[24] While the drive to return to the past may be a knee-jerk response to the 2019–22 pandemic, it is possible for schools to prepare for the next disruption, with a proactive approach to adapting to and embracing changes that can function to improve schools at the same time.

Schools are guided by the policies developed by system managers, who are gatekeepers when they fail to deviate in any way from a fixed course of action. If a strategic plan has been revised on an ongoing basis, it needs to be aligned with the school improvement plan. A quality strategic plan should be a path out of one condition into an improved "new" reality.

This chapter highlighted some key issues related to policies and funding in schools. While it did not address questions related to transportation, meal support, and each policy populating dense school procedural manuals, it did present some considerations for examining existing policy and funding practices with a fresh lens. By considering alternative perspectives, it is possible to gain a deeper understanding of school practices, often taken for granted.

The world has many competing policies, some more dire than others: the metric system vs. the imperial system, where to place the steering wheel on a car, and the size of paper for printers are not as serious as the collision of democratic and communist ideals. Nevertheless, a global education should not rely on universal standards. There is strength in diversity, and without diverse schools with diverse populations, there are inherent weak links in a system that supports uniformity.

It's not about creating a school—it's about creating new systems that support innovative school directions. Lab schools should not be so rare; they should not be confined by the testing practices in schools they are mandated to improve upon.

The worshipping of school policies as fixed procedures that drive schools on the same industrial road without any built-in flexibility to feature innovation, beyond the wires, boxes, and often replicated technological software, is not working. Policy should respond to vision, not be the vision in a school. To increase student and teacher engagement, policy and school budgets must support significant change in schools. It is possible for policies to support more creative schools, better equipped to do more than push out the same sausage in the same schools every day.

"You can use logic to justify almost anything. That's its power. And its flaw."

–Captain Cathryn Janewa

NOTES

1. V. Hughes (2022, September 15), Convenor, The Sensible Centre.
2. K. Bartlett (2022, October 13), LinkedIn, https://www.linkedin.com/feed/update/urn:li:activity:6986460299302162432/.
3. E. C. Sheninger (2016), *Uncommon learning: Creating schools that work for kids*.
4. S. Burosch (2017), The head, the hands and the heart: A conversation with John (Jack) Miller, The Mehrit Centre, https://self-reg.ca/the-head-the-hands-and-the-heart/.
5. Burosch, The head, the hands and the heart.
6. B. Freud (2022, November), https://www.linkedin.com/posts/benjaminfreud_pluriverse-activity-6989118893583654912-IBNk/?trk=public_profile_like_view&originalSubdomain=ch.
7. A. Thiruselvam (2022, October 20), Singapore has among the world's best education systems, so what can Australia learn from it?, ABC News, https://www.abc.net.au/news/2022-10-21/how-australia-can-compare-to-singapore-education/101511316.
8. S. Braybrook (2022, October 16), principal's desk, Facebook.
9. D. B. Reeves (2020), *The learning leader: How to focus school improvement for better results* (2nd ed.).
10. Hughes, Convenor.
11. Hughes, Convenor.
12. R. Wilson & S. McGrath-Champ (2022, August 4), The conversation.
13. B. J. Smith (2023, in press), *Teacher shortages and the challenge of retention: Practices that make school systems and cultures more attractive and empowering*.
14. B. J. Smith (2023), *Assessment tools and systems: Meaningful feedback approaches to promote critical and creative thinking*.
15. B. J. Smith (2021), *How much does a great school cost? School economies and school values*.
16. J. Reich (2020), *Failure to disrupt: Why technology alone can't transform education*, p. ix.
17. Reich, *Failure to disrupt*.
18. D. Buck (2022, September 24), Twitter.
19. R. Lewis (2022, October 15), The principal's desk, Facebook.
20. S. Khan ([AU: year?]), The Guardian Institute.
21. Sheninger, *Uncommon learning*.
22. Smith, *How much does a great school cost?*

23. Smith, *How much does a great school cost?*
24. R. Owen (2022, April 21), Can we make real, transformative change in education? *Greater Good Magazine*, https://greatergood.berkeley.edu/article/item/can_we_make_real_transformative_change_in_education.

Further Discussion
Embrace the Storm

The idea of *Star Trek* required the fictional characters to not only storm the wall separating discovery from sameness but embrace such a path of most resistance. If improvement is to happen in schools, real stakeholders need to find a way to embrace the storms that will form when different forces try to occupy the same school space.

Schools are not serving everyone; it doesn't matter what kind of school, the critical mass of unknowing, uncaring, under-stimulated, and discouraged students is too many, and no matter how hard the teachers try, it is the system that holds them down. In *Star Trek: The New Generation*, the "Borg" was a worthy opponent for Captain Jean-Luc Picard. The creation of a villain as an elaborate cyber system mirrors and rivals the fixed operations of schools today. Like fiction, too many gatekeepers may pretend to embrace change in education, but few are willing to get wet; that is, to go somewhere where few have gone before, to be a part of the storm.

Unravelling the fixed designs of schools takes more than a dose of leadership courage; it requires policy that makes room for exploration. Storms are required to disrupt the normal pattern of schooling, but they do not need to change every school and every teacher at the same time. School systems can and should create laboratory schools, without the chains of testing. Just as starships were not meant to stay put, school systems should be planning for change.

Accountability measures were created to manage the system that exists, not one that has yet to be discovered. Checks and balances for traditional school systems were developed for fixed and familiar expectations of schools. New schools should not be driven by policies of current schools; otherwise, it's a façade to pretend that what is being designed is "new."

A simple response to the burning question—"How then, would such 'new' systems be accountable?"—is that they won't be. A more comprehensive school design would mean that qualitative descriptions of meaningful and relevant experiences would emerge as education would no longer be subject to standardized comparisons. Rather, schools would be learning spaces where standards are applied in creative and engaging ways; just as no two people or two communities are the same, no schools should be alike. This is precisely the route to school improvement; this way education ships can remove the anchors of testing handcuffs to outdated systems.

Before doing any more backward designing from the present school model, there needs to be a disruptive storm that enables innovation and creativity to forge new paths; gatekeepers must embrace change on a large systematic scale. The guest authors invited to share their perspectives in this journey were selected because they found a way to leave the monotonous educational orbit. They stormed the gates of traditional schooling, whether situated in the United States, Canada, the Netherlands, or Australia. They navigated paths in their various roles and opportunities around and within their various systems. To risk moving schools beyond their current flight path, these trailblazers not only needed to recognize the entrenchment of gatekeeping in education systems but also do something about it.

There are many writers and educational experts who have informed thinking about new ways to do education. Blended within this text are many incredible global voices who share experiences beyond the limited orbits of traditional schools.

Rick Wormeli challenged us all to think carefully about the assumptions surrounding testing, and the value of more comprehensive feedback. Author of the bestseller, *Fair Isn't Always Equal*, Rick's positive spirit and vision presents a balanced look at the limitations of standardized testing, as well as the benefits of quality feedback. Fellow Americans Bena Kallick and Allison Zmuda from the Habits of Mind Institute shared compelling ideas to enlighten readers about the need to develop four attributes of a personalized culture for learning (voice, co-creation, social construction, and self-discovery).

Continuing with the theme of mindful teaching and learning, Ted Spear, founding Head of the Island Pacific School in Canada, added much food for thought about the memory-making capacity of his school's "Masterwork's classes." His book *Education Re-imagined* features a host of powerful student-driven transformative stories. University of Toronto graduate student and expert outdoor educator Emily Walton Doris reminded readers that experiential learning and the value of educating in and about the outdoors should be an option in a quality school experience.

The chapter on finding and preparing staff to meet the diverse needs of students and engaging curriculum, was followed by Australia's Michael Lawrence's account of his experiences in Finland, a country where teachers are valued in society. His book, *Testing 3, 2, 1: What Australian Education Can Learn from Finland* examines what Finland did differently from Australia and how the culture contributed to Finland being heralded as top of the education game, worldwide. Trusting teachers and students is at the root of a good education.

Following the chapter examining school forces, founder, owner, coach, and consultant of *Thrive, Structuring for Success*, Luke Coles, addresses the notion of team over faculty. An experienced school administrator, Luke promotes a culture of autonomy and transparency through a shared responsibility organizational model featuring the idea of "students-at-the-core" and a collective analysis using a spectra tool for staff reflection.

Teacher-leader Tanisha Nugent Chang from Washington, DC, shares her perspective as a mathematics coordinator and Dean of Teacher Development in a charter school for the performing arts. Her "hands on" coaching helped to support teachers and build a vibrant team of teacher-leaders. Responding to the chapter about leadership in schools, John Neretlis, Head of the Brick Labs Academy in Toronto, shared highlights of how he navigated around many gatekeepers to open a new school, dedicated to community, joy, and learning in the context of a Science, Technology Engineering, and Mathematics (STEM) school context.

Seasoned author, consultant, and founder of Creative Leadership Solutions, American Douglas Reeves from Boston, addressed the serious concern of censorship as a gatekeeping action. His comparison of US and Chinese educational systems shielding students from "essential truths" is compelling. His ideas caution educators to allow for critical analysis; after all, it is the source of an educated strong citizenry.

In a comprehensive review of gatekeeping in higher education, consultant and member of the Ontario College of Teachers' Accreditation Committee, Beverley Freedman, shared insight into the limited access and barriers associated with a university education for all students. Both explicit and implicit examples are presented of what challenges must be met as students from refugee and immigrant families try to find the invisible steps to higher education.

Author and consultant Cap Lee, from Milwaukee, Wisconsin, shared the article "Saving Students from a Shattered System" in response to the chapter "House of Mirrors." Lee de-mystifies the notion of equality, acknowledging the deep-rooted problems of sameness, and viewing students through blurred lenses. This powerful piece challenges accepted norms and offers viable solutions to support a whole education so that each child can achieve "their maximum potential."

Each guest author focused on a key issue in education that they addressed in a creative and thoughtful manner. Aware of the limitations of fixed gates, they each found ways to navigate around various barriers to improvement. What makes the news related to education, however, tend to be the issues that could be coined as the great gatekeeping distraction.

THE GREAT DISTRACTION

When a system is committed to perpetuating the system, it can often benefit from actions that distract stakeholders from significant change. Taking away a teacher's right to strike for instance, by defining them as "essential workers," distracts not only the taxpayers, but the teachers, as well. Teachers who work in schools without unions have individual contracts, without the option to strike; in many of these cases salaries are also much lower than the teacher wages in public systems.

Contracts in independent and charter schools are usually offered on a year-to-year basis; whereas public systems negotiate terms over several years, making it challenging to anticipate pay with varied costs of living. Ideally, teachers should be paid decent wages so they can afford not simply housing, but food and recreational activities, with benefits like any other college graduate. The reality, however, is that too many teachers need part time jobs to make ends meet. Many talented teachers are leaving the profession.

The staffing of human capital in schools needs to change, but collective agreements are based on fixed staffing formulas. While teachers will strike for more pay, it is rare for strike action to be dedicated to revising roles and responsibilities. Furthermore, there is little attention paid to the lack of supports and mentors to help teachers in the field, nor enough time to plan for quality teaching and learning. Gatekeepers have much to gain when the focus of negotiations remains on the right to strike and increased pay, diverting attention away from the need for significant systematic change. As long as the participants in collective agreements are distracted, few changes in schooling will happen.

Nevertheless, teacher pay is a road block to school improvement and needs to be addressed in a more substantial way than playing catch-up in contract negotiations in three- to five-year cycles. The determination of teacher pay and benefits, relative to planned increases over multiple years in the future, can be an engineering nightmare. Trying to anticipate fiscal and benefit needs takes up enormous time and energy. Do taxpayers really need to listen to communications politicizing different sides of contract debates? Could such funds be better utilized for adding more teachers in schools to support student learning?

A starting point would be to adjust base salaries to make them more attractive for teachers in the profession. If teacher wages and benefits began close to a six-digit salary and increased or stayed the same based on the cost of living, there might be less need for the "crystal ball" analysis and assumptions underlying projections for future needs. When teachers are renewing their contracts, it should not be a simple matter of a percentage pay increase.

When the cycle and priorities of employment contracts can be disrupted, there can be more time dedicated to fight such fights as classroom size, school size, and the need to remove the emphasis on standardized testing in schools. Unfortunately, the collateral impact of an increase in salary is also an increase in the number of students in each classroom. When collective agreements are viewed as a percentage increase negotiation, teachers are often forced to choose work conditions that are counter to quality teaching and learning.

Another key distraction muddying the waters for school change is the exaggerated claim of learning loss during and following the recent pandemic. The testing sirens sounding such alarms have much to gain from data walls that show that students were unable to soak in as much content as they could do prior to the COVID lockdowns and closures. The curriculum was overcrowded before, during, and after the pandemic crisis. The opportunity to determine what was essential, by fine tuning curriculum, did not mean that students will be less prepared for college, the world of work, or life. No testing company can make such absolute assumptions.

In Canada, the province of Ontario handed out coupons for families to supplement education with tutors to help students "catch up." The funds allocated for such vouchers would be better spent on increasing the number of teachers in schools and reducing the number of students in classrooms. Pandemic or not, all students in schools have not been experiencing a learning gain, ever since testing became the priority in schools. Coupons are band-aids to much more serious systematic problems in schools today. The hype about "learning loss" is a distraction from doing the hard work necessary to make systematic change a reality.

Finally, the budget in any educational system is a gatekeeping tool, especially if the line items are fixed and projected spending is approved based on patterns of former budgets. Even if the school system needs improving, budgets tend to follow a predictable path. If decision-makers are serious about improving education for all students, then budgets must also be open for change.

Boards of education often operate as fiscal mangers, rather than visionaries. The budget, or the pattern of budgets past, tends to drive the work of school trustees. Rather than supporting and even co-designing a better direction for education, the process of budgeting itself becomes a distraction from improvement. Some board members in schools may examine executive summaries of quantitative data comparing test scores, attendance, or student enrollment, but few will address qualitative long term plans for more comprehensive school improvement.

The access to dashboard software that serves up glossy pages of simple-to-read numbers for school trustees is available on demand. Attending a board meeting can be as convenient as ordering from a fast-food menu on

Doordash or Uber Eats. The testing industry has made it easy for those at the top of the school food chain to be distracted by scores that have never proven to improve teaching and learning.

In Holt's classic work *How Children Fail*, he warns that "school is a place where children learn to be stupid," further suggesting that "Children come to school curious" and "within a few years most of that curiosity is dead, or at least silent." How is that such a concern is still valid today? Concerned about students in the 1960s being bored in schools, Holt claimed students do tasks with only a small part of "attention, energy, and intelligence," adding "this soon becomes a habit," getting used to "working at low power." Educators, as Holt noted, "tell ourselves that this drudgery, this endless busywork, is good preparation for life, and we fear that without it children would be hard to control."[1]

INTEREST GROUPS: REPRESENTATIVES OF VOICE AND CHOICE

In education there are many interest groups that support specific missions of their organizations, and in doing so, a few assume responsibility for the interest of many. Teaching unions and federations, for instance, are responsible for negotiating the collective agreements, detailing the contractual expectations of the teaching employees. Groups representing non-instructional employees play an important role in schools, as well.

While these voices tend to be some of the most powerful interest groups in education, there are others who can play an influential role either through their action or inaction. Some well-intentioned groups may collect under the umbrella of Facebook groups such as "Cultivating Happier Schools," "School Success Makers," or "The Principal's Desk." Some may gather on LinkedIn:

- 21st Century Education
- Early Childhood Education
- School Leadership 2.0
- Leadership Think Tank
- International Education Forum
- STEAM Connections for K-12
- ASCD
- OISE Alumni
- International School Educators
- Professional Education Networking
- Assessment for Change
- Big Ideas in Education

The list of communities one can join can seem endless. Access to experts and those who share similar passions can happen on many media fronts including live podcasts, webinars, YouTube, and TedTalks.

Some groups exist to promote a fixed view of schooling. They use words like accountability as weapons fiercely focused on results and testing scores assuming that the system is fixed, not evolving or improving. Groups that place so much emphasis on ranking students and schools have an arrogant notion of what a school must be. Groups of education management companies, for instance, tend to invest in cookie-cutter schools that can scale their operation.

To be fair when determining ranking designations, all schools and school systems must follow the same blueprint, assuming all students will respond to the script in the same way. Furthermore, the purpose of school is not to be like other schools. The purpose is to educate minds that can not only understand the present but have the capacity to solve problems that currently have no solution.

Given that the answer to the earth's sustainability is not on page 431 in a textbook or an option of a, b, c, or d on a multiple-choice test, educators must break free from the limits of ranking, to allow creative and critical thinking to take shape in unique and distinct learning contexts. Imagine if we placed trust in every student to have the potential to cure cancer? Society must stop fussing about inflated grades, mastery, or whether to drop a student's grade because their work was handed in late. Students have too many serious challenges to prepare for, and school systems must embrace the research that grounds the need for significant change.

The press is a force that can also play a role in gatekeeping or "gatestorming." It's easy, convenient, and less controversial to write a story about student test scores and ranking. It takes deep investigative reporting skills to see that data walls and ranking lists are distractions to bring the public on board as gatekeepers, guards pretending to protect an outdated system that operates under the premise that one-half of all students will not meet learning expectations.

Probably the most dangerous interest groups are those that sit on the fence. These bystanders choose not to be on the bold side of history. They may fear reprisal if they "like" a bold comment on LinkedIn or Twitter, or they may think that being in the middle of issues is a safe place to be. Often it is said that those watching the storm do not want to get wet; they prefer to let others be disruptors, even though they may be well informed about grounded research.

Too many gatekeepers working in Departments or Ministries of Education and in teacher preparation and even graduate programs have succumbed to accepting a middle ground position. Such positions should be filled by change agents, not passive bystanders. It should not be okay to let educational theory and research evaporate above the boiling curriculum stew filled with everything imaginable from the grocery store. When managers are in charge, the purpose of schooling is about compliance and replicating sameness; positions of responsibility need to be occupied by leaders who empower teachers and students to choose the ingredients to design an engaging and authentic learning meal.

The world of testing has prompted many more controls than what existed over half a century ago. Testing forces have influenced a dominant culture in schools. By reducing teaching time and student-driven learning, busy work cloaked in a disguise of technology has contributed to a new wave of stupidity, one sadly devoid of much engagement. Gladwell claimed that "Cultural legacies are powerful forces. They have deep roots and long lives."[2] While it may take time to generate new cultures, it is important for school systems to change, adapt, and improve.

So, what's worth storming the fixed gates of schools and school systems? And why should the gatekeepers in school systems rethink resisting change? The "inspiring learning experiences" listed below represent at least reasons to embrace change, as well as fifty empowering and grounded experiences schools miss out on when gatekeeping actions prevent and hinder growth. According to Pink: "For talent to grow, bureaucracy must wither."[3]

INSPIRING LEARNING EXPERIENCES IMPEDED BY GATEKEEPING ACTION

1. Inspired, creative, confident, and joyful learners
2. Proactive wellness programs ensure schools are healthy communities.
3. Educators and school staff are paid well with ample benefits.
4. Maximum fourteen students in classes with smaller numbers in specialized elective classes
5. Calendar in synch with the rest of world (Monday is Monday, not Day 3 or 8 . . .)
6. Reduced school hours—kids and teachers sleep in—more time for extra-curricular experiences; lesson-free days
7. Reduced number of more rigorous expectations; emphasis on "power" or "essential" standards
8. 90 minute+ time slots to increase teacher:student interactions; application and research
9. Inter-disciplinary projects and only two to three subjects at one time in middle and high school (i.e., Semestering)
10. Splitting of heavy content courses in high school over two years to permit for micro-courses/micro-credentialing

11. Middle and high school students experience two- and three-year "extended studies" and "research"
12. Value and celebrate critical and creative thinking and action in authentic contexts
13. Personalized culture for learning; individualized learning plans for all students
14. Adapting and creating new approaches and systems that support a "whole child" education
15. Project Based Learning; "Habits of Mind," "Experiential Learning," "Design Thinking," peer teaching (i.e., SHARK Inquiry), students as authors, "Masterworks" classes, apprenticeships (i.e., Launch Program)
16. Commitment to compassion, relationships, and collaborative learning conditions
17. Life skills with community service is a key learning context
18. Arts, outdoor education, athletics valued as key intelligences (i.e., "Hour in—Hour Out" school day . . .)
19. Student leadership roles for all (i.e., yearbook editors, Playground Leadership Project, Model UN)
20. Freedom to debate with a deep understanding of social justice; challengers of status quo are respected
21. Technology is integrated as part of the twenty-first and twenty-second-century pencil case
22. Balance of student-driven individual and collaborative learning (no demand for tutoring industry)
23. Option to attend micro-schools, Laboratory schools, Forest Schools . . . with 300 or less students
24. Principals, other admin, special ed staff, librarians, and tech staff have partial teaching roles
25. Use of student and staff portfolios, interviews, collection and explanation of artifacts as collecting evidence of learning that reveals "mastery" and "criterion based" learning; no standardized tests or test preparation curricula
26. Use of simplified and fair assessment systems (i.e., A [ample evidence]; B [some evidence]; NY [not yet any evidence]); removing excess verbiage and integrated self-assessment on rubrics
27. Distinct and attractive physical and natural school environments
28. Strategic plans where many stakeholders embrace the messiness of change
29. Not afraid to admit and learn from mistakes "fail forward"
30. All stakeholders have opportunity to generate strategic/school improvement plans

31. More teacher leaders and fewer educators reporting to only a few school leaders
32. Customized professional learning (i.e., team teaching, team planning for collaborative curriculum design)
33. Regular book study/action research days/sabbaticals built into schedule
34. Positive peer pressure (e.g., using "Spectra Review Tool" . . .)
35. Teachers have autonomy to share passions and construct resources
36. Unit or term planning designed by teachers, not commercially designed products
37. Use of both quantitative and qualitative data to inform decisions and actions
38. Parents, staff, and students use survey outlets to balance voices/choices and perspectives (i.e., "Students-as-Core" Organizational Structure . . .)
39. Home study with family as co-researchers and inquirers (e.g., Family Projects)
40. More time for parent-teacher-student conferences as teacher has fewer students
41. News media features more cases of qualitative evidence from schools/systems
42. Exposure of parents, students, and teachers to innovative approaches/experiences/research in education
43. Faculties of education as incubators of free thought and innovation, lead the challenge to update school systems
44. University educators have equitable status (i.e., removal of multi-tiered hierarchies . . .)
45. Experts in higher education make time to read, endorse, and respect practitioner work
46. Higher education has affinity groups, peer mentors, financial subsidies, affordable housing, and childcare
47. Peer-reviewed journals accept narrative accounts as well as include practitioner writing
48. Case studies, action research, participatory research, and ethnography have increased status
49. Community college is linked to work and university
50. Reciprocity of teacher and leadership credentials across state/provincial and national borders

Education is indeed a complex organization that often seems overwhelmed by the gatekeeping mechanisms that keep schools moving in a backward motion. The good news is that there are mavericks and outliers who have challenged the status quo and explored new ways of doing school. This sampling of "Inspiring Learning Experiences" does not pretend to capture the full picture of what many stakeholders miss out on in schools, but it also highlights the brave who have taken risks to go where few schools have gone before.

Who are the gatekeepers and who are the stakeholders who should be storming the gates to improve schools and systems? They are the same people: governmental officials, education experts, faculties of education, graduate schools, school accreditors and authorizers, publishers, school leaders, Directors of Education, central office staff, teachers, teacher unions/federations, professional associations, politicians, trustees, parents, students, and community members. Each stakeholder has the power to improve or not.

When school leaders and board members remove their testing blinders, they will be able to understand that more data will not improve school systems; people will. Data walls and viewgraphs full of charts and spreadsheets can keep school leaders and trustees distracted with the busy work of trying to interpret them. The hard work, however, comes when all those responsible for education take the time to learn about quality education, and in so doing, be brave enough to be designers of better systems, not caretakers of a bridge to nowhere.

"Without freedom of choice there is no creativity."

—Captain James T. Kirk

And without creativity, there can be no change; there can be no improvement.

NOTES

1. J. C. Holt (1964), *How children fail.*
2. M. Gladwell (2014, October 22), Outliers and cultural legacies, https://www.culturalfront.org/2014/10/outliers-cultural-legacies-chapter-6.html
3. D. Pink (2022, October 11), Twitter.

References

@north1963. (October 16, 2022). Twitter.
Akhar, T. (September 20, 2022). LinkedIn.
Altwerger, B., & Strauss, S. (2002). The business behind testing. *Language Arts, 79*, 256–263.
Aleven, V., & Koedinger, K. R. (2002). An effective metacognitive strategy: Learning by doing and explaining with a computer based cognitive tutor. *Cognitive Science, 26*, 147–179.
Anvi. (2021, May 12). How academia & its jargons gatekeep knowledge & uphold class-caste divide. Feminism in India. https://feminisminindia.com/2021/05/12/academia-jargon-gatekeep-knowledge-class-caste-divide/.
Arnold, K. (October 16, 2022). Twitter.
Atkinson, R. K., Renkl, A., & Merrill, M. M. (2003). Transitioning from studying examples to solving problems: Effects of self-explanation prompts and fading worked-out steps. *Journal of Educational Psychology, 95*, 774–783.
Atwal, K. (October 12, 2022). The Thinking School. Twitter.
Audrain, L. (October 15, 2022). Twitter.
Bargh, J. A., & Schul, Y. (1980). On the cognitive benefit of teaching. *Journal of Educational Psychology, 72*, 593–604.
Bartlett, K. (October 13, 2022). LinkedIn. https://www.linkedin.com/feed/update/urn:li:activity:6986460299302162432/.
Bearison, D. J., Magzamen, S., & Filardo, E. K. (1986). Sociocognitive conflict and cognitive growth in young children. *Merrill-Palmer Quarterly, 32*(1), 51–72.
Beekes, W. (2006). The "millionaire" method for encouraging participation. *Active Learning in Higher Education, 7*, 25–36.
Benware, C. A., & Deci, E. L. (1984). "Quality of learning with an active versus passive motivational set." *American Educational Research Journal, 21*,755–765.
Bielaczyc, K., Pirolli, P., & Brown, A. L. (1995). Training in self-explanation and self regulation strategies: Investigating the effects of knowledge acquisition activities on problem solving. *Cognition and Instruction, 13*, 221–251.
Bleske, B. (February 26, 2019). The Absurd Structure of High School. GEN. https://gen.medium.com/the-insane-structure-of-high-school-762fea58fe62.

Bloom, B. S. (1968). Learning for mastery. *Evaluation Comment* (UCLA-CSIEP), *1*(2), 1–12.

Bossert, S. T. (1988). Cooperative activities in the classroom. *Review of Research in Education, 15*, 225–252.

Brown, A. L., & Palincsar, A. S. (1989) Guided, cooperative learning and individual knowledge acquisition. In L. B. Resnick (Ed.), *Knowing, learning, and instruction: Essays in honor of Robert Glaser* (pp. 393–451). Lawrence Erlbaum Associates, Inc.

Braybrook, S. (October 16, 2022). Principal's Desk Facebook Group.

Buck, D. (September 24, 2022). Twitter.

Burosch, S. The head, the hands and the heart: A conversation with John (Jack) Miller. The Mehrit Centre. https://self-reg.ca/the-head-the-hands-and-the-heart/.

Canadian Accredited Independent School (CAIS). https://www.cais.ca.

Canadian Bureau of International Education (2022). The student voice: National results of the 2021 CBIE international student survey. https://km4s.ca/wp-content/uploads/CBIE_2021_International_Student_Survey_National_Report.pdf.

Ms. Carasco. (October 12, 2022). Twitter.

Chi, M. T. H., & Bassock, M. (1989). Learning from examples via self-explanations. In L. B. Resnick (Ed.), *Knowing, learning, and instruction: Essays in honor of Robert Glaser.* (pp. 251–282). Erlbaum.

Chi, M. T. H., Bassock, M., Lewis, M., Reimann, P., & Glaser, R. (1989). Self-explanations: How students study and use examples in learning to solve problems. *Cognitive Science, 13*,145–182.

Chi, M. T. H., de Leeuw, N., Chiu, M. H., & LaVancher, C. (1994). Eliciting self-explanations improves understanding. *Cognitive Science, 18*, 439–477.

Chi, M. & VanLehn, K. A. (2010). Meta-cognitive strategy instruction in intelligent tutoring systems: How, when and why. *Journal of Educational Technology and Society, 13*, 25–39.

Coburn, C. E. (2001). Collective sensemaking about reading: How teachers mediate reading policy in their professional communities. *Educational Evaluation and Policy Analysis, 23*(2), 145–170. https://doi.org/10.3102/01623737023002145.

Cole, D. (October 12, 2022). Twitter.

Common Application. https://www.commonapp.org.

Council of International Schools (CIS). https://www.cois.org/.

Daily Maverick. (October 14, 2022). Twitter.

DC Public Charter School Board. https://dcpcsb.org.

Deal, L. (October 12, 2022), Twitter @lpdeal.

Devlin, M. (October 15, 2022). Twitter.

Dill, D. (October 13, 2022). Twitter.

Director, Civil Society Australia. Convenor. The Sensible Centre. https://www.abc.net.au/news/2022-10-21/how-australia-can-compare-to-singapore-education/101511316.

DPI. (November 30, 2021). Program Launches Students on Careers. PDI. https://dpi.wi.gov/news/dpi-connected/program-launches-students-careers.

Downes, S. (2005). An Introduction to Connective Knowledge. Stephen's Web.

Drake, S. M. (2012). *Creating standards-based integrated curriculum: The common core state standards edition, 3rd edition.* Thousand Oaks, CA: Corwin.

Duncan, D. (2005). *Clickers in the classroom: How to enhance science teaching using classroom response systems.* San Francisco: Pearson/Addison-Wesley; 2005.

Easey, K. (September 12, 2022). LinkedIn.

Florida Language Arts Standards, Third Grade. https://cdn5-ss14.sharpschool.com/UserFiles/Servers/Server_270532/File/Students%20&%20Parents/Grades%20and%20Graduation/Elementary/LAFS_WIDA_ThirdGrade_Ataglance.pdf

Florida Language Arts Standards, Fourth Grade. https://drive.google.com/file/d/1Il6ufKayzYSJoDsgIoU61vs07z3n6LFh/view.

Florida Language Arts Standards, Fifth Grade. https://cdn5-ss14.sharpschool.com/UserFiles/Servers/Server_270532/File/Students%20&%20Parents/Grades%20and%20Graduation/Elementary/LAFS_WIDA_FifthGrade_Ataglance.pdf.

Freud, B. (November 2022). https://www.linkedin.com/posts/benjaminfreud_pluriverse-activity-6989118893583654912-IBNk/?trk=public_profile_like_view&originalSubdomain=ch.

Friedman, J. (2022). Banned in the USA: The growing movement to censor books in schools. PEN America 100. https://pen.org/report/banned-usa-growing-movement-to-censor-books-in-schools/.

Fullan, M. (Summer 2007). Change the terms for teacher learning. Thought Leader. National Staff Development Council. 28 (3). http://michaelfullan.ca/wp-content/uploads/2016/06/13396074650.pdf/.

Fullan, M., & Rizzotto, J. (2022) When it comes to the teacher shortage, who's abandoning whom? https://michaelfullan.ca/wp-content/uploads/2022/10/When-It-Comes-to-the-Teacher-Shortage-copy.pdf.

Furze, L. (2022, October). LinkedIn. https://www.linkedin.com/posts/leonfurze_breaking-out-of-teel-activity-6985060758984302594-lWP8/?trk=public_profile_like_view&originalSubdomain=au.

Gassaway, W. (October 12, 2022). Twitter @WendyGassaway.

Gavrielatos, A. (October 16, 2022). Reddit. https://www.reddit.com/r/AustralianTeachers/comments/xxmhop/nsw_day_of_action_october_12th/..

Gladwell, M. (October 22, 2104). Outliers and Cultural Legacies. https://www.culturalfront.org/2014/10/outliers-cultural-legacies-chapter-6.html.

Graesser, A. C., McNamara, D., & VanLehn, K. (2005). Scaffolding deep comprehension strategies through AutoTutor and iSTART. *Educational Psychologist, 40*, 225–234.

Greene, P. (July 21, 2021). What's the matter with for profit charter school management? *Forbes.* https://www.forbes.com/sites/petergreene/2021/07/21/whats-the-matter-with-for-profit-charter-school-management/?sh=2d1d7bc77a3e.

Guskey, T. R. (August 18, 2016). New Directions in the Development of Rubrics. http://tguskey.com/new-direction-in-the-development-of-rubrics/.

Hargreaves, A. (October 12, 2022). Twitter.

Harvard Project Zero. https://pz.harvard.edu/.

Mrs. Hernandez. (October 17, 2022). Twitter @Mrs.Hernandez322.

High Tech High. (2022). Tijuana and HTH students exhibit co-created magazine. https://www.hightechhigh.org/tijuana-and-hth-students-exhibit-co-created-magazine/.

High Tech High. (2023). Projects. https://www.hightechhigh.org/student-work/projects/.

Holt, J. C. (1964). *How children fail.* Dell Pub. Co.

Hughes, V. (September 15, 2022). Convenor, The Sensible Centre.

International Baccalaureate (IB). https://www.ibo.org.

Jane Katkova & Associates. Now it is official. Canada is the most educated developed country in world! https://canadianimmigrationexperts.ca/canada-is-the-most-educated-developed-country-in-world/.

Jude. (October 13, 2022). Twitter.

Kallick, B. (September 15, 2022), LinkedIn.

Kallick, B., & Zmuda, A. (2017). Personalized culture for learning. https://files.ascd.org/staticfiles/ascd/pdf/siteASCD/publications/books/students-at-the-center-sample-chapters.pdf.

Khan, S. The Guardian Institute.

King, A. (1992). Facilitating elaborative learning through guided student-generated questioning. *Educational Psychologist, 27*, 111–126.

Kit. (October 12, 2022), Twitter.

Knight J. K., Wise S. B., & Southard, K. M. (2013). Understanding clicker discussions: Student reasoning and the impact of instructional cues. *CBE-Life Sciences Education, 12*, 645–654.

Kohn, A. (September 9, 2022). Twitter.

Kohn, A. (September 27, 2022). Twitter.

Kohn, A. (2007). Rethinking homework. https://www.alfiekohn.org/article/rethinking-homework/.

Ladwig, L. (October 20, 2022). Twitter.

Lain, S. (2017). Poetry is not out of the box. *New England Reading Association Journal, 52*(1), 20–25. https://www.proquest.com/docview/2405313561.

Lasry, N., Mazur, E., & Watkins, J. (2008). Peer instruction: From Harvard to the two-year college. *American Journal of Physics, 76*(11),1066–1069.

Lave, J., & Wenger, E. (1991). *Situated learning: Legitimate peripheral participation.* Cambridge University Press. https://doi.org/10.1017/CBO9780511815355.

Lawrence, M. (2020). *Testing 3, 2, 1: What Australian education can learn from finland.* Melbourne Books.

Lee, E. C. (2019). *Stop politically driven education: Subverting the system to build a new school model.* Rowman & Littlefield.

Leung, A. (October 15, 2022). Twitter.

Lewis, R. (October 15, 2022). The Principal's Desk. Facebook Posting.

LinkedIn Job posting. https://www.linkedin.com/jobs/view/head-of-school-pretty-river-academy-at-lhh-knightsbridge-3272677652/?utm_campaign=google_jobs_apply&utm_source=google_jobs_apply&utm_medium=organic&originalSubdomain=ca.

Lopez, A. (September 13, 2022). Twitter.

Lucas, A. (2009). Using peer instruction and i-clickers to enhance student participation in calculus. *Primus, 19*(3), 219–231.
Lucas, M. (October 12, 2022). Twitter.
Lucy. (September 14, 2022). The Principal's Desk. Facebook Group.
Luther, M. (October 12, 2022). Twitter.
Lynn, S. (October 13, 2022). Twitter.
Mann, C. (October 12, 2022). Twitter.
Mazur E. (1997). *Peer instruction: A user's manual.* Prentice Hall.
McDermott, G. (October 13, 2022). Twitter.
Middle States Accreditation (MSA). https://www.msa-cess.org.
Minton, W. (October 29, 2019). What Bill Gates doesn't understand about supporting teachers. LinkedIn. https://www.linkedin.com/pulse/what-bill-gates-doesnt-understand-supporting-teachers-william-minton/.
Morbius, A. (October 12, 2022). Twitter.
National Association of Independent Schools (NAIS). https://www.nais.org.
Noddings, N. (1985) Small groups as a setting for research on mathematical problem solving. In E. A. Silver (Ed.), Teaching and learning mathematical problem solving (pp. 345–360). Erlbaum.
Novinger, S., & Compton-Lilly, C. (2005). Telling our stories: speaking truth to power. *Language Arts, 82*, 195–203.
Owen, R. (April 21, 2022). Can We Make Real, Transformative Change in Education? *Greater Good Magazine.* https://greatergood.berkeley.edu/article/item/can_we_make_real_transformative_change_in_education.
Paterson, C. (September 12, 2022). Timetable Absurdity. Getting Smart. https://www.gettingsmart.com/2022/09/12/timetable-absurdity/.
Patrick, Not Pat. (October 11, 2022). Twitter, @PresidentPat.
Patrick, Not Pat. (October 14, 2022). Twitter, @PresidentPat.
Pink, D. (October 11, 2022). Twitter.
Porter, L., Bailey-Lee, C., & Simon, B. (2013). *SIGCSE '13: Proceedings of the 44th ACM technical symposium on computer science education.* ACM Press, pp. 177–182.
Priniski, J. H., & Horne, Z. (2015). Crowdsourcing effective educational interventions. In A. K. Goel, C. Seifert, C. Freska (Eds), *Proceedings of the 41st annual conference of the cognitive science society.* Austin: Cognitive Science Society.
Ravitch, D. (2022, October 12). PEN America: The growing movement to ban books. https://dianeravitch.net/2022/10/12/pen-america-the-growing-movement-to-ban-books/.
Rees, J. (2001). Frederick Taylor in the classroom: standardized testing and scientific management. *Radical Pedagogy,* (3), 2. Retrieved on June 15, 2021, from http://radicalpedagogy.icaap.org/content/issue3_2/rees.html
Reeves, D. B. (2011). Getting ready for common standards. *American School Board Journal* (March). https://drive.google.com/file/d/1l16ufKayzYSJoDsgIoU61vs07z3n6LFh/view.
Reeves, D. B. (2020). *The learning leader: How to focus school improvement for better results* (2nd ed.). ASCD.

Reeves, D. B. (February 1, 2021). Five professional learning transformations for a post-COVID world. ASCD, *78*(5). https://www.ascd.org/el/articles/five-professional-learning-transformations-for-a-post-covid-world.

Reich, J. *Failure to disrupt: Why technology alone can't transform education* (ix). https://cmsw.mit.edu/failure-to-disrupt-why-technology-alone-cant-transform-education/.

Renkl, A., Stark, R., Gruber, H., & Mandl, H. (1998). Learning from worked-out examples: The effects of example variability and elicited self-explanations. *Contemporary Educational Psychology, 23*, 90–108.

Resnick, L. B. (Ed). *Knowing, learning, and instruction: essays in honor of Robert Glaser* (pp. 393–451). Erlbaum.

Richards, T. (1997). *The meaning of Star Trek: An excursion into the myth and marvel of the star trek universe.* Doubleday.

Richards, W. (October 12, 2022). Twitter.

Ritchhart, R., Church, M., & Morrison, K. (2011). *Making thinking visible.* Jossey Bass Wiley.

Rittle-Johnson, B. (2006). Promoting transfer: Effects of self-explanation and direct instruction. *Child Development, 77*, 1–15.

Robichaud, A., & Chomsky, N. (2014). Interview with Noam Chomsky on education. *Radical Pedagogy, 11*(1).

Rockwell, D. (October 12, 2022). Twitter.

Ryskin, R., Benjamin, A. S., Tullis, J. G., & Brown-Schmidt, S. Perspective-taking in comprehension, production, and memory: An individual differences approach. *Journal of Experimental Psychology: General, 144*, 898–915.

Sanchez, Morgan. (October 16, 2022). Twitter.

Shafiyeva, U. (August, 2021). Literacy and standardized testing. *Literacy Letters*.

Sheninger, E. C. (2016). *Uncommon Learning: Creating Schools that Work for Kids.* Thousand Oaks: Corwin.

Sidebottom. (October 11, 2022). Twitter,

Siemens, G. (2005). Connectivism: Learning as network creation. http://www.astd.oeg/LC/2005/1105_siemens.htm.

Simply Hired (October 2022). Head of school with liberal arts education. Estero Classical Academy. https://www.simplyhired.com/search?q=school+principal+jobs&l=florida&job=RsMXqQPfVNE95YAZyOb4Ai49-SWi61DvnWUzpwx7xehkr1jMi5zyOA.

Smith, B. J. (2017). *A charter school principal's story: A view from the inside.* Sense Publishers

Smith, B. J. (2021). *How much does a great school cost? School economies and school values.* Rowman & Littlefield.

Smith, B. J. (2022, in press). *Assessment tools and systems: Meaningful feedback approaches to promote critical and creative thinking.* Rowman & Littlefield.

Smith, B. J. (2023, in press). *Teachers shortages and the challenge of retention: Practices that make school systems and cultures more attractive and empowering.* Rowman & Littlefield.

Smith, B. J., & Blecher, H. (2023, in press). *Write to be read.* Rowman & Littlefield

Spencer, J. (2022). PBL by design—Exploring the overlap of project-based learning and design thinking. https://spencerauthor.com/pbl-by-design/.

Spillane, J. P., & Zeuli, J. S. (1999). Reform and teaching: Exploring patterns of practice in the context of national and state mathematics reforms. *Educational Evaluation and Policy Analysis, 21*(1), 1–27. https://doi.org/10.3102/01623737021001001;

Steinbeck, J. (1939). *The grapes of wrath*. New York: The Viking Press.

Storey, S. (October 15, 2022). Twitter.

Sullivan, K. (October 14, 2022). Twitter.

Talk Project, https://www.goodreads.com/book/show/12949036-classroom-talk.

The Marigold Project. (October 14, 2022). Twitter.

Thiruselvam, A. (2022, October 20). Singapore has among the world's best education systems, so what can Australia learn from it?. ABC News. https://www.abc.net.au/news/2022-10-21/how-australia-can-compare-to-singapore-education/101511316.

Thomas, D. (1952). *Do not go gentle into that good night*. https://poets.org/poem/do-not-go-gentle-good-night.

Timperley, H. S., & Phillips, G. (2003). Changing and sustaining teachers' expectations through professional development in literacy. *Teaching and Teacher Education, 19*(6), 627–641.

Tirozzi, G. N., & Uro, G. (1997). Education reform in the United States: National policy in support of local efforts for school improvement. *American Psychologist, 52*(3), 241–249. https://doi.org/10.1037/0003-066X.52.3.241.

Tullis, J. G., & Goldstone, R. L. (2020), Why does peer instruction benefit student learning?. *Cognitive Research: Principles and Implications, 5*. https://www.ncbi.nlm.nih.gov/pmc/articles/PMC7145884/.

Tutt, J. (October 13, 2022). Twitter.

UBC. https://recreation.ubc.ca/2019/02/07/what-is-storm-the-wall/.

VanLehn, K., Jones, R. M., & Chi, M. T. H. (1992). "A model of the self-explanation effect." *Journal of the Learning Sciences, 2*(1), 1–59.

Vedder, P. (1985). *Cooperative learning: A study on processes and effects of cooperation between primary school children*. Rijkuniversiteit Groningen.

Vygotsky, L. S. (1981). The genesis of higher mental functions. In J. V. Wertsch (Ed.), *The Concept of Activity in Soviet Psychology* (pp. 144–188). M. E. Sharpe.

Wagner, K (September 12, 2022), Linkedin.

Dr. Watson. (October 17, 2022). Twitter, @terrinwatson.

Webb, N. M., & Palincsar, A. S. (1996). Group processes in the classroom. In D. C. Berliner & R. C. Calfee (Eds.), Handbook of educational psychology (pp. 841–873). New York: Macmillan Library Reference USA: London: Prentice Hall International.

Williams, S. (May 25, 2022). Facebook message.

Wilson, R., & McGrath-Champ, S. (August 4, 2022). The Conversation.

Wong, R. M. F., Lawson, M. J., & Keeves, J. (2002). The effects of self-explanation training on students' problem solving in high school mathematics. *Learning and Instruction, 12*, 23.

Wormeli, R. (2018). *Fair isn't always equal*. Stenhouse Publishers.

Yackel, E., Cobb, P., & Wood. T. (1991). Small-group interactions as a source of learning opportunities in second-grade mathematics. *Journal for Research in Mathematics Education,* 22, 390–408.

York University. Assistant professor, literacy in early childhood education, faculty of education. York University. https://www.yorku.ca/edu/about/current-opportunities-literacy-in-early-childhood-education/.

www.ingramcontent.com/pod-product-compliance
Lightning Source LLC
Chambersburg PA
CBHW022013300426
44117CB00005B/163